The Adventurers

About the author

Anthea Masey is a financial journalist who has worked for publications such as *Which?* magazine, the *Investors' Chronicle* and the *Daily Mail*. As a freelance writer she contributes to the *Mail on Sunday*, the *Independent* and the *Herald*. She co-wrote with Sir John Harvey Jones the bestselling *Troubleshooter* which was published by BBC Books in 1990. Anthea Masey lives in London with her husband and two children.

THE ADVENTURERS

A Year in the Life of a Venture Capital House

Anthea Masey

BBC BOOKS

This book is published to accompany the
television series of the same name
which was first broadcast in February 1993

Published by BBC Books,
a division of BBC Enterprises Limited,
Woodlands, 80 Wood Lane, London W12 0TT

First published 1993
© Anthea Masey 1993

ISBN 0 563 36771 7

Designed by Gwyn Lewis

Set in Mono Lasercomp Calisto
by Selwood Systems Ltd, Midsomer Norton

Printed and bound in Great Britain by
Butler & Tanner Ltd, Frome and London
Cover printed by Clays Ltd, St Ives plc

Contents

Acknowledgements

I would like to thank all those who are mentioned in this book, companies as well as individuals, for their help and co-operation in checking and rechecking facts and figures and for the time they gave up to be interviewed. In particular, I must thank everyone at Grosvenor Venture Managers for their support; series producer Anne Laking and producer Bill Grist at BBC Television; and at BBC Books, commissioning editor Heather Holden-Brown and editor Vanessa Daubney for keeping me sane.

Anthea Masey

Introduction

During the last months of 1991 and most of 1992, the television cameras were the fly on the wall of Grosvenor Venture Managers. They carefully watched and recorded as Grosvenor's executives painstakingly considered dozens of potential deals. The process provides a unique insight into venture capital and the essential mystery of how deals are done. In each case it illuminates the drama behind the figures, the psychological dimension, the forging of new relationships, in a way which no dry textbook, however informative, can ever achieve.

In 1992 Grosvenor reached its tenth year. It employed eight investment executives and by the middle of that year it had invested a cumulative £75 million in 107 companies. Funds under management at this time were around £60 million in 56 companies which when compared with other venture capitalists puts Grosvenor in the medium-sized league.

In this book you will meet the various Grosvenor executives who do the deals and look after the investments. The work of a venture capitalist is extraordinarily varied; one day they could be looking at the blanket industry, the next they could be worrying about proposed EC emission levels from incinerators, or the effect Nigel Mansell's world championship win will have on sales of motor racing videos.

Most decisions as to whether or not to invest in a company are arrived at by a sort of informal consensus. However, each executive brings his or her own interests and prejudices to bear and this can lead to occasional differences of opinion. For example, some executives start by looking at the price of the deal and the rate of return and, if these look right, they will recommend backing a business almost regardless of what it does; while there are others who look first at the nature of the business and its potential for growth. But in the end both approaches are brought to bear on the final decision.

You will also meet the entrepreneurs who approached Grosvenor for finance. All needed venture capital to expand their businesses. Some were only just starting out; others were aiming for rapid expansion; others had sound businesses which were simply running out of money. And in these recessionary times there were two cases of managers trying to buy their companies from the receiver. Some had turned to venture capital after banks had rejected them as too risky.

All were affected in some way by their experience of seeking venture capital. For some it was a true rite of passage into a new phase of their business career. It can take months to finalize a venture capital deal and the wait can be agonizing. Entrepreneurs can never count on the deal being done until the money is actually in their company's bank account. Most started celebrating as soon as Grosvenor said it was prepared to back their business. But that was only the beginning of a long, drawn out and often complex set of negotiations during which the shape, structure and value of the deal could, and often did, change quite radically. Few venture capital deals go through in a completely straightforward fashion; most go through what the venture capitalists describe as the white knuckle phase. Many entrepreneurs felt it would have been helpful to know in advance how others had fared before them, a need which this book should help to remedy.

Grosvenor is a venture capitalist which likes to take an active role in the management of the companies in which it invests and talks a lot about developing partnerships with those companies. But it can be the case that those companies which are keenest on developing such a management partnership are actually the least likely to persuade venture capitalists to back them. Some of the companies featured in this book were, initially, ambivalent about the management role Grosvenor intended playing. However, once these relationships were established, they were universal in their praise of Grosvenor's ability to steer a middle course helping them to improve their management skills while leaving the entrepreneur free to grow the business.

It is often argued that in Britain our financial institutions are way ahead of the rest of Europe but that our businesses lack the marketing and production skills of our main competitors. It is certainly true that in Britain we have the largest venture capital industry outside the United States, but is it backing the right businesses, will it put its money behind the truly profitable business idea, and does it have a role to play in restructuring industry? Hopefully the experience of the venture capitalists and entrepreneurs in this book will contribute something to this debate.

As an aid to understanding some of the terminology used there is a glossary at the end of the book. Asterisked words refer to this.

Chapter One

Venture Capital

Venture capital is often confused with banking, and while it is true that venture capitalists and bankers are both in the business of providing money to industry, it's about the only thing they do have in common. If banking is like diving for pennies in a swimming pool, then venture capital is like diving for gold off a high cliff when you don't know if the water is six inches or sixty feet deep.

Bankers make their profits by borrowing money from one set of people in order to lend it to another set at a higher rate of interest. Venture capitalists do it differently; instead of lending money, they take an unsecured stake in the companies they back and they only make money when a company is successful, a process which can take many years of careful nurturing.

Venture capital is all about risk. The main function of venture capital is to make profits for investors by providing funds for small- and medium-sized enterprises, many of which are unwilling or unable to raise money in more conventional ways. If venture capitalists could predict which companies were going to succeed, they would all retire as millionaires. But it is the nature of the beast that for every real winner backed by venture capital there are likely to be a number which go bust and yet more which struggle on going nowhere in particular.

Bankers earn their money at regular intervals in the form of interest. Venture capitalists have to wait a lot longer, and they never really know how much money they have made on any particular investment until they sell it. This can happen when a company they have invested in is sold to another company, or it has reached the stage where it is strong enough to get a stock market listing and the shares can be sold to the public.

It is a fact of venture capital life that money tends to be lost before it is made. The companies which are going to go bust tend to do so in the first year or so after receiving the attentions of the venture capitalist, but with the successful ones it can take anything from three to ten years before the venture capitalist actually sees a profit.

Today most venture capital companies are owned by the big banks, pension funds and merchant banks who have decided to commit a slice of their funds to venture capital. Others are independent and responsible for raising their own investment funds. There are even a few individual business angels: wealthy individuals who like the idea of rolling up their sleeves and putting their money and expertise at the service of someone else's small business to help get it off the ground. The Body Shop's Anita Roddick was able to start her first shop in Brighton by selling a share in the company to a local Littlehampton garage owner, Ian McGlinn, for £4000 – an investment which is now worth around £95 million.

But wherever they work, there is a commonly held notion in the industry that venture capitalists are born not bred. This book accompanies the BBC television series, *The Adventurers*, which charts the progress of some of the deals made or investigated during a year in the life of Grosvenor Venture Managers, an independent venture capital operation which in the early 1980s started life by managing the rump of the National Enterprise Board's investments in small companies in what was effectively one of the very first privatizations of the Thatcher government.

Robert Drummond, Executive Chairman of Grosvenor Venture Managers, says it is easier to define venture capitalists by what they are not rather than by what they are:

'They are not bankers. Bankers lend money for relatively low returns so can't risk losing it.

'They aren't merchant bankers. Merchant bankers are deal-driven; they earn their money from fees – the more

deals they do, the more they earn. Venture capitalists may charge fees but it is not the driving force or the motive for doing the deal.

'Nor are they industrialists. Industrialists want to control everything. Venture capitalists keep a close watch on the companies in which they invest. They normally insist on having a non-executive director on the board, but the aim is to provide the kind of guidance and help which doesn't crush the entrepreneurial drive that attracted the venture capitalist to the company in the first place.

'They aren't investment managers in the normal way either. Most investment managers don't have to develop the skills to nurture the companies in which they invest.

'The venture capitalist is characterized by a certain independence of spirit and it isn't until someone actually starts doing it that you know whether or not they possess that essential quality. Those that don't usually leave the industry pretty quickly.'

The history of venture capital is probably as old as enterprise itself. The merchant adventurers of the middle ages sunk their fortunes into ships which roamed the world in search of trade and sometimes plunder. The East India Company, which controlled trade with India for nearly two centuries, could trace its origins back to these early, privately financed ships, and even those overseas traders which are still around today, such as Jardine Matheson and Sime Darby, although not as old, will admit to similar buccaneering beginnings if pressed.

Britain's pre-eminence during the early stages of the industrial revolution was undoubtedly due partly to the willingness of rich individuals to finance and develop the inventions of Crompton and Arkwright in the Derbyshire textile industry and the work of the great engineers such as Stephenson and Brunel.

The wealth this generated led to the export of capital which financed the building of much of the world's railways. By the end of the nineteenth century it was becoming increasingly common for individuals to club together to form syndicates which went exploring for investment opportunities overseas, particularly in North America. Many of the trusts founded in these years, such as Foreign & Colonial and Scottish Investment Trust are still around today and form the foundation of what is now the £25 billion investment trust industry.

So venture capital has a long, if somewhat swashbuckling past. However, for much of the early years of this century, with one or two notable exceptions, venture capital was more the exception than the rule and it was hardly the well established and accepted activity that it is today.

The modern model of venture capital was pioneered by Charterhouse in the 1930s when the bank started providing finance for small and growing companies by taking a direct equity stake. The next significant development came after the war when the Bank of England and the English and Scottish clearing banks set up the Industrial and Commercial Finance Corporation (ICFC) to provide a source of long-term capital to British industry – mainly to small- and medium-sized companies which do not have ready access to other forms of capital. ICFC, renamed 3i (Investors in Industry), is now the country's largest venture capital organization by far with a network of 23 local offices and total funds managed of £2.5 billion.

The venture capital explosion which took place during the 1980s was clearly driven by the boom conditions and the new spirit of enterprise which prevailed throughout much of the Thatcher decade. But its development also has connections with the more interventionist approach of the previous Labour government whose criticism of the financial community for its lack of support for entrepreneurs operating in high risk areas, particularly technology, led to the formation of state-run organizations, such as the National Enterprise Board, and the Welsh and Scottish Development Agencies, all of which made available venture capital funds.

Venture capital grew at a phenomenal rate during the 1980s both in terms of the number and variety of organizations offering this sort of finance, but also in the number of deals done and the amount of money invested. In 1980, there were only around 20 sources of venture capital funds. By the end of the decade the membership of the British Venture Capital Association (BVCA)* had grown to 122, and there were probably a further two dozen organizations operating outside the BVCA.

Britain's venture capital industry is now the largest outside the United States. In 1991 BVCA members invested £1153 million in 1386 companies. This was well down on the record set in 1989 when the industry invested £1647 million in 1569 companies. But figures for earlier years – in 1981 for example, the industry lent just £66 million to 163 companies – show just how far the industry has progressed over the last decade or so.

Much of this success can be explained by the popularity of management buy-outs*, a type of finance which many in the industry would argue is not venture capital in its truest sense.

To the purist, venture capital is the provision of equity finance* to emerging and small enterprises and involves a high degree of risk for the potential of a very high reward. A management buy-out is where the managers of an existing business arrange to buy it from the owner, normally a larger company which has decided to concentrate on its other interests. The management pay for the company by borrowing money and selling some of the company's shares to a venture capitalist.

Management buy-outs work best with profitable, medium- to large-sized companies with a well proven track record. This is quite distinct from most other forms of venture capital. In theory at least, management buy-outs involve a low level of risk. This has little to do with what most people see as venture capital's primary function which is to provide equity finance to companies which are still a long way from seeking a stock market quote* and which, in some cases, may not be much more than a gleam in the entrepreneur's eye.

The popularity of management buy-outs provided much of the growth in venture capital right up until the end of the 1980s when it became clear that many of the larger management buy-outs which had been structured with excessively high levels of debt were experiencing difficulties in meeting their interest payments.

Since 1987, management buy-outs have taken the lion's share of venture capital investment. In 1983 they accounted for a quarter of all venture capital investment. By 1991 the proportion was 55 per cent having reached a peak of 61 per cent in 1989. However, these figures mask the fact that the large, heavily geared management buy-outs which were such a feature of the last overheated years of the 1980s have now totally disappeared from the financial scene. In fact, the overall decline in the amount of venture capital investment over the last three years is almost entirely accounted for by the decline in the amount provided to management buy-outs which fell from £867 million in 1989 to £544 million in 1991.

Venture capitalists turn up in the most surprising places. The industry itself categorizes firms as either independent or captive. The independents are just that – they don't belong to a bank, pension fund or stockbroker – and they must raise their investment funds independently on the back of their reputation. 3i, in spite of being owned by the big clearing banks, is categorized as an independent and, as we have already seen, is the largest provider of independent venture capital funds. At the other end of the independent spectrum there are a few firms, like Birmingham Technology (Venture Capital), which specialize in investing quite small amounts in companies that are still virtually on the drawing board.

Most of the money raised by the independents is invested via unquoted investment funds, most of which have a fixed life – usually ten years – after which the money is returned to investors.

Some independents choose to raise part or all of their funds through quoted investment trusts* so that their investors can sell their shares as and when they want. The money is raised in the first place mainly from institutional investors, although there is nothing to stop private investors who want to invest in venture capital from buying the shares too. However, they have to bear in mind that in venture capital, while there are fortunes to be made, there are also fortunes to be lost; it all depends on the skill of the manager and the nerves of the investor.

Five years ago there were 13 quoted investment trusts specializing in venture capital. Of these only four beat the *FT* Actuaries Index. Candover, the management buy-out specialist, did particularly well returning £3374 for every £1000 invested over the five years to the end of 1992. Three out of the 13 actually managed to lose money for their investors. The wooden spoon over this period goes to Sumit which managed to lose £740 for every £1000 invested.

In a move pioneered by the British Coal pension funds, the last ten years have seen the emergence of captive venture capital organizations operating as separate entities within banks, insurance companies, merchant banks and other financial institutions, and reliant on them for funds. The move was prompted probably more by self-interest than any criticism that the banks in particular were failing their small business customers. The banks saw they were losing customers, and potentially rich pickings, because not only were they failing to provide venture capital finance but they had also not developed the skills needed to operate in this very specialist field.

All the big four clearing banks, Barclays, Lloyds, Midland and NatWest, now have in-house venture capital operations, as do most of the major merchant banks, including Barings, Rothschilds, Schroders and Warburgs. Some big insurance companies, notably Eagle Star, Legal & General, Prudential and Sun Life also commit funds to venture capital.

But perhaps most surprisingly, there are still small amounts of venture capital available from government agencies such as the Welsh Development Agency, Scottish Enterprise and the Tayside Enterprise Board which have survived the government's itch to privatize.

It is a romantic view of venture capital to think that here is a source of funds tripping over itself to lend to every white-coated boffin with a bright idea. There are funds available for developing technological and scientific ideas with commercial potential, but such early stage finance* – often called seed finance* – is extremely hard to obtain and few venture capitalists specialize in this area as many frustrated scientists can confirm.

The reasons are not hard to find. Venture capitalists are in the business to make money for their investors, and this sort of early stage finance is extremely risky. Most seed corn money gets spent with nothing to show for it at the end except shattered dreams.

In fact, all early stage finance, including money for starting up companies and for loss-making young businesses, represents a considerable risk for the venture capitalist. Most companies in this category will also require considerable management support from the venture capitalist if they are to succeed.

It is hardly surprising to find that most venture capitalists prefer backing companies which have an established track record. Providing such companies with funds for expansion is by far the most popular proposition to put before a venture capitalist. In 1991, out of the 1262 deals logged by members of the BVCA, only 273 involved early stage finance. And although management buy-outs take most of the money, they don't predominate when it comes to the number of deals. In 1991, 529 companies succeeded in raising venture capital finance for expansion, while the number of management buy-outs and buy-ins* was actually only 288.

Chapter Two

Grosvenor

Grosvenor's chairman, Robert Drummond, tells a story from his early days as a venture capitalist twenty years ago which demonstrates the importance of psychology to the venture capitalist:

'I can't even remember the company because it isn't what the company did, or even what happened to it, which has stuck in my mind. All I know is that it taught me a useful lesson.

'I put forward a package of loan and share capital which I was almost certain would be accepted because the terms were fairly favourable. Yet the owner stubbornly refused to sign and I couldn't understand why. It wasn't until he made some chance remark about being a millionaire that I realized the deal just failed to give him that kudos.

'It was clearly very important to him, so I tinkered with the deal. He didn't even mind us having a larger share in his business. What he wanted was to be able to say that he was a millionaire – giving him the pleasure of being able to say that enabled me to do the deal.'

Grosvenor celebrated its tenth birthday in 1992. As an independent venture capital company, Grosvenor doesn't rely on one particular bank or financial institution for its funds.

Grosvenor was created as a private investment vehicle when the government decided that the National Enterprise Board's smaller investments in unquoted companies should be sold. The National Enterprise Board (NEB) was created by the last Labour government which took the view that the state had a role to play in the restructuring of industry and the nurturing of small companies. The National Enterprise Board was meant to be one of the main instruments of this industrial strategy. However, by the early 1980s it became clear that the Thatcher government was determined to wind down the NEB. It was David Beattie, at that time a NEB director, who came up with the idea of effectively privatizing a number of small unquoted investments by spinning them off into a private investment fund. Originally it was not intended that he should go with them, and it wasn't until John Oakley, the industrialist and company doctor*, was appointed as chairman, that it was decided to bring David Beattie in as chief executive.

The NEB had its headquarters in Grosvenor Gardens, near London's Victoria Station, which is how the name Grosvenor came to be attached to what was effectively the privatization of the NEB's venture capital investments.

Independent venture capital funds, as Grosvenor was destined to become, normally raise their investment funds in the City from institutions such as pension funds, insurance companies and investment trusts. In the UK private investors play only a small part in providing venture capital funds. Grosvenor raised £6.9 million from three major City institutions and the NEB injected its venture capital assets in exchange for a quarter share in the new fund. This was some time before Robert Drummond joined Grosvenor but as he says they didn't inherit the crown jewels.

Of the eight NEB investments four were disasters. The rest did reasonably well. For example, a £250 000 investment in Thandar, which made electrical measuring equipment and which had once formed part of the NEB's investment in Sir Clive Sinclair's company Sinclair Radionics, eventually realized £560 000; an investment of £700 000 in Sonicaid, a company making medical ultra sound equipment, made a profit of £400 000, and a very modest investment of £20 000 in the engineering company, Powerdrive, was eventually sold for £610 000. However, the one real star was more a matter of luck than judgement. This was Burndept a company in radio communications. The shares, which were brought for £650 000, were initially sold at a loss to a company called FKI, extraordinarily a mini-conglomerate that Robert helped create by two management by-outs in the late 1970s whilst he was at 3i. However, Grosvenor hung on to its shares in FKI which subsequently did very well. When Grosvenor eventually sold them several years later, it had made a profit of £1.7 million.

The NEB was renamed the British Technology Group (BTG) and continued to licence its high technology investments. In March 1992, BTG was privatized with the management and staff doing a management buy-out from the government and history turned a full circle with Grosvenor investing £500 000 for a six per cent stake.

By all accounts 1985 was a significant year for Grosvenor. Most of the £6.9 million of new money raised at the time of the buy-out from the NEB had been invested and Grosvenor's investors were well pleased with the results so far.

It was time to ask them for some more money. But venture capital was then taking off in a big way in the UK and two of Grosvenor's investors wanted to manage their own operation from then on.

This gave David Beattie and his team the opportunity they had been looking for to run their own independent management company. They had already formed a small shell company which they renamed Grosvenor Venture Managers. It was quickly agreed with their own employers, Grosvenor Development Capital, that this vehicle should have the contract to manage the existing Grosvenor fund and that it should raise more money to manage in a new and separate fund. Thus David and his colleagues became shareholders in the company and so were fully motivated to build their own business through good times and bad.

Grosvenor's second tranche of money was called the Grosvenor Technology Fund, or second fund, as it is frequently known within the company. It attracted £9.5 million of new money. As a hangover from its NEB days, Grosvenor has a reputation for understanding technology, of which it is proud. Grosvenor is by no means only interested in technology-based companies, but Robert Drummond is convinced that they still get offered some of the best technology deals.

There have been several further fund raising rounds. In 1988, the Third Grosvenor Fund more than doubled its predecessor when it raised £21.7 million. And the following year Grosvenor raised the Grosvenor International Investors Fund, or fourth fund as it is often called. The money for this fund came from overseas investors, mainly in the US, for investment in the UK. The fund raised £7.4 million and has put its money largely into the same investments as the third fund.

At the end of 1989, the huge success of Sage, a computer software company, and one of Grosvenor's best investments, contributed to Grosvenor being able to raise further money. Sage had decided to go public, but this presented the first fund, Grosvenor Development Capital, with a huge capital gains tax problem since it had run out of the tax shelter provided by its loan stock. Most of the original investors in the fund were tax-exempt pension funds which deeply resented having to pay the tax. Grosvenor got round the problem by floating the fund on the stock market as an authorized investment trust, a status which brings with it freedom from capital gains tax. This provided the opportunity to extend Grosvenor Development Capital's activities by simultaneously raising £10 million of new capital – the first time a venture capital trust had raised new money of this order.

By the summer of 1992 Grosvenor had decided to approach its investors with a suggested target of £60 million for a new fund that would be available to invest over the later years of the recession and hopefully the first year or so of recovery. Displaying the optimism of all good venture capitalists the directors talked of a first closing of the fund by the end of November. So, with not even the palest of green shoots of recovery showing, Grosvenor was out there again testing the investors' appetite for venture capital.

The cyclical nature of venture capital means that there are times when it is either difficult to raise new money, or the money available for investment is better off in the bank because the deals which are on offer are either of poor quality or over priced or both. This is particularly the case for the independents who cannot rely on regular flows of new funds from a helpful parent. Venture capital investors are as prone to following the herd as any other group of investors investing heavily when funds are plentiful and deals expensive and staying away when funds dry up and deals are cheap. The ease with which Grosvenor raised that £21.7 million in 1988, just at the point when the management buy-out boom reached fever pitch before the bubble burst, is a case in point. But then investment is not an entirely rational business which is why there are opportunities for those brave enough to put their jobs on the line and go against the herd to invest when all around is doom and gloom and prices look cheap.

Venture capital is all about doing enough good deals to pay for all the deals which either go wrong or go nowhere in particular, the so called living dead*.

There is no doubt that Grosvenor can point to some early successes. In 1984, as mentioned previously, it invested in Sage, a tiny software company which had spotted the potential for a simple accounting programme for the smaller business and also had anticipated the pricing development that changed the whole structure of software distribution. This is an example of just how profitable early stage finance can be if the company succeeds. Sage is now a public company and was worth over £110 million at the beginning of February 1993. Grosvenor made a profit of £9.1 million and both the company's founders, David Goldman and Graham Wylie, are now wealthy men.

Another early success was the management buy-in of computer services company, Marcol, in 1983 which has made a profit of £6 million for Grosvenor. Marcol is a good example of the doctrine of getting under the skin of your entrepreneur. In 1990, Dr John Rigg, the driving force behind the Marcol deal, brought the management buy-in of Vega, the space systems company, to Grosvenor. Two years later when Vega Group plc was floated on the stock market, Grosvenor made a profit of nearly £2 million. And now Grosvenor is backing Dr Rigg's newest enterprise, Triad Special Systems, a company which designs computer systems for government departments and local councils.

The stresses and strains of the constant fund-raising, and the never ending stream of deals to be looked at which characterized the late 1980s, may have taken their toll on David Beattie's health.

After he was unwell in the autumn of 1989, it was agreed to recruit a new managing director to reduce the day-to-day pressure on David. Robert Drummond was appointed and the two worked in tandem for a year: Robert Drummond as managing director; David Beattie as executive chairman of Grosvenor Venture Managers. Sadly it wasn't a partnership which was to last. A year later, in the summer of 1991, at the age of 52, David Beattie died and Robert took over as chairman.

Robert Drummond's career in venture capital goes back 20 years and if there were such a thing as a venture capital gene, then Robert Drummond surely has it. His father, Guy Drummond, was the very first executive recruited by ICFC when it was formed in 1945, so venture capital and later, when his father took to company doctoring, entrepreneurship, were part of the culture of his childhood.

Robert Drummond learnt his venture capital craft following in his father's footsteps at ICFC, by then renamed 3i, where he ended up running the all important south east region. He then spent five years building up County NatWest's venture capital operation before joining Electra.

County NatWest was not always an harmonious place to work. The Blue Arrow scandal had poisoned working relationships within the merchant bank long before Robert Drummond decided to leave. But it wasn't just the Blue Arrow affair: he was also frustrated by the merchant banking culture which is driven by the need to earn fees and is entirely alien to the philosophy of venture capital. He said:

'I had managed to assemble a group of people who understood venture capital, but I'm not sure the rest of the bank ever really understood what I was trying to do. In the end I decided I would be happier working for an independent.'

Robert went to work for Electra, the quoted venture capital fund, but was frustrated by his inability to influence decisions there:

'When I was offered the chance to join Grosvenor and take a 20 per cent stake in the management company it was an

opportunity too good to miss. Here, I am able to influence the way the place is run and how it is to develop. I also benefit financially if it goes well.'

Independent venture capitalists will only survive if they can establish a good performance record. Venture capital investors have to be prepared to tie up their money for at least five years, and they need to be able to reassure themselves that the eventual returns will justify their patience. And while it is true that those fund managers who tough it out and invest during a recession are likely to do best over the long term, it is at times like these when the actual performance figures look their worst.

The fact that Grosvenor's early funds have performed well while the later ones are still finding their feet demonstrates both the long-term nature of venture capital and the exceedingly difficult investment climate which has prevailed since 1988.

But these are early days for the last two funds and whereas in the mid-1980s the average time it took for a venture capital investment to reach maturity narrowed to just a couple of years, the gap has now widened again, and no one expects a quick return any more. There is also no doubt that the performance of these two funds would be a great deal worse if Grosvenor had got caught up in the management buy-out mania which saw companies like Magnet and Isosceles, the Gateway food chain, emerge with giddily high levels of debt and a frightening exposure to any upturn in interest rates or downturn in trade, both of which subsequently happened.

Venture capital doesn't always get a good press, with criticism levelled at high fees and deals which many entrepreneurs say are loaded in favour of the venture capitalist. How do these criticisms look from the inside? Robert Drummond mounts a stout defence of all charges of profiteering:

'There are always going to be people who feel aggrieved, although a recent survey shows that 98 per cent of entrepreneurs backed by venture capitalists – even those that failed – were satisfied. Even in a recession we get a constant flow of people knocking on our door. In 1992 we made 4

investments. **We would have seriously investigated many times that number, weeded out from nearly 500 enquiries,** so from this you can see that there are a lot of people around who probably feel that venture capital has failed them because they have failed to persuade anyone to back their business.

'We occasionally get letters of complaint from people we have turned down claiming that a particular executive has mistreated them in some way. I'll want to know why, but I will almost invariably congratulate the executive on his or her good judgement as well. Businessmen worth their salt don't waste their time complaining, they are too busy exploring other avenues of finance.

'It is a fact of venture capital life that the good deals have to pay for all the deals which go wrong, and it is this element of cross subsidy which occasionally makes the entrepreneur think we are trying to pull a fast one on them. However, we have to keep reminding them, that if we are aiming for a rate of return on our investment of, say, 32 per cent a year, then this assumes that the owner will soon be a millionaire.

'I warn people against paying fees to venture capitalists. Some are greedy and will ask for them but unless the venture capitalist is leading a syndicate of investors, and putting the deal together has involved a lot of work, then they are usually hard to justify. Entrepreneurs who are charged fees for straightforward venture capital deals should challenge them and if they don't get a satisfactory answer they should seriously think about going elsewhere for their funds.

'I'm not denying that some businessmen haven't been bruised in their brushes with venture capitalists. But there have been several instances of investors having been persuaded to put large amounts of money into speculative companies with virtually no safeguards.'

The case of biotechnology company Porton International is an example. In 1983 and 1985 the company persuaded various city institutions to invest a total of £76 million in Porton on the basis that it was developing an anti-herpes drug which was forecast to generate profits of £128 million by 1989. Nothing came of the drug, and losses mounted until the chairman, Wensley Haydon-Baillie, brought in John Burke as chief executive from Glaxo. He has recently turned the company round from a loss of £7.8 million in 1990 to profits of £6 million in 1991.

And then there are the deals which are often brought to venture capitalists but which on closer analysis aren't really suitable. They are the 'lifestyle' deals. Here the venture capitalist is often approached when a further injection of money is needed to prop up the entrepreneur's standard of living. Robert Drummond says:

'There is nothing wrong with businessmen using venture capital to release cash for themselves, but it should never be the main motivation behind the deal. A sudden jump in living standards can be very demotivating, the very opposite of what the venture capitalist is trying to achieve.'

And there are the 'equity gap' companies – so called because the amount of money they are seeking to raise is so small that no one is interested in backing them. Robert Drummond explains why he thinks the equity gap is largely illusory:

'It doesn't make sense for us to invest £50 000 or £100 000, it's just not economic. The amount of management time we spend is as great, if not greater, with a company in which we invest £100 000 as it is with one in which we invest a million. If small companies really had confidence in themselves they would think big and ask for more money. We are looking at an ambition gap, not an equity gap.

'It is this concept of partnership which is at the core of venture capital and which separates it from all other forms of finance. If we can get over to the entrepreneur that this is not a "them and us" relationship, but a very real partnership in which we will normally have representation on the board and we will be on hand with help and advice without in any way interfering with the day-to-day running of the business, then we have won half the battle.'

In the summer of 1992, Robert Drummond took on the job of chairman of the British Venture Capital Association. Up until then he had combined the roles of chairman and chief executive of Grosvenor Venture Managers. The decision was taken to split the two jobs. Robert remained as chairman and Michael Glover moved up to become the new managing director. It was not an arrangement that lasted. In early December 1992 it was decided that Michael's talents were best employed looking after Grosvenor's existing investments. He is now working as a consultant and continues as a director of Grosvenor Venture Managers. And Grosvenor has decided not to replace him as chief executive.

When 53-year-old Michael Glover left university in 1960 with a degree in economics he decided he wanted to work in industry but in a sector which was dynamic and growing. He chose the electronics industry and landed a job with Elliott Automation. He spent much of the sixties working at the cutting edge of the newly emerging integrated circuit and computer industries.

There then followed a period when Michael worked for a number of North American electronics companies helping to set up companies in the UK and the Far East. Returning from a two-year stint in Singapore he became a management consultant, a move which eventually brought him into contact with David Beattie at Grosvenor. He explained:

'One of my clients asked to be put in touch with sources of venture capital. Grosvenor then asked me if I would help them evaluate any electronics proposals which came to them and it all led on from there. When David Beattie was thinking about raising the second fund in 1984, he asked me to join the team. Helping companies to grow and finding them sources of finance was what I had been doing as a consultant so it seemed a natural progression to pop round to the other side of the table.'

His future career as a venture capitalist was sealed.

Tony Crook has the longest association with Grosvenor. In 1980 he was hired by David Beattie at NEB to implement his proposal to spin off the NEB's unquoted investments into what became

Grosvenor. He continued to be employed by the NEB while working for Grosvenor, during which time he raised the £6.9 million for the Grosvenor fund. This arrangement came to an end in 1982 when he finally joined the staff of Grosvenor.

It was as much Tony's decision to site Grosvenor's offices in Slough as it was David Beattie's. He offered the company's reasons for this: 'Apart from the desire to keep down costs, we wanted to distinguish ourselves from other venture capitalists who are mainly based either in the City or the West End.'

At the age of 56, Tony Crook has been in venture capital for over twenty years. Like many people he stumbled into it by accident. An early career in sales, marketing and general management had made him think that what he liked best was being involved with smaller businesses as a whole:

'I started looking for a job in merchant banking but at that time in my mid-thirties I found I fell between two stools; I was neither the bright young thing straight out of university or the experienced industrialist. It was around this time that I saw an advertisement for a job in venture capital and I realized it would suit me better.'

Having spent twenty hard-working years in venture capital, Tony is now trying hard to carve out more time to himself. A keen real tennis player – he drinks his tea from a mug bearing the motto 'old tennis players never die' – he wants to spend more time on the tennis court, on the golf course and reading the books he has never read. However, he still looks after around a dozen of Grosvenor's investments, being on the board of six of them, and he is still committed to two days a week working on general Grosvenor Venture Managers business.

Bill Edge, who is also 56, as well as being a director of Grosvenor Venture Managers is also the longest serving Grosvenor employee having been with the company right from the beginning in 1982. Bill concentrates on looking after Grosvenor's existing investments and he has responsibility for around 15 of these. He also keeps a watchful eye on some of the younger, less experienced executives, as they weigh up the investment proposals which come in.

23

On the wall in Bill's office there is a strikingly colourful poster for Edges Dolly Dyes. This is a nostalgic relic from the Edge family archive. Bill was the fifth generation of Edges to join the family household chemical business. He came to venture capital relatively late after a long career in business. When the family household chemicals company was sold to Reckitt & Colman in 1967 Bill, who didn't fancy the life of a multi-national executive, worked as a management consultant. He then worked in the pharmaceutical industry and finally managed the industrial investments of a large paper importer. Bill says that a business background can be a great help to the venture capitalist: 'We have a lot more understanding of the problems of the general manager trying to grow his company than someone who has been in a bank and is trying to look after a few investments from a City office.'

Thirty-three-year-old Janis Anderson grew up in Africa where her father worked in public administration in various countries. She read economics at Manchester, but instead of a safe, well paid job in the City, she took herself off to the other side of the world to Bermuda where she worked for the Bank of Bermuda for a couple of years.

Even when she returned to London her work and her contacts continued to be overseas. She worked for Meridian International, a privately financed bank, where she invested in projects in the developing world, especially Africa. Her progress to venture capitalist came via a conscious decision to find a job which would put an end to her wanderings and would have a European focus. Three years spent in the corporate finance department of accountants Robson Rhodes eventually led to a job at Grosvenor and at the beginning of 1992 she became the first ever Grosvenor employee to make the grade to director and shareholder of Grosvenor Venture Managers, the management company.

Lance Phillips, who at 28 was one of Grosvenor's youngest and newest employees, joined the company from Harvard Business School in the summer of 1991. Venture capital was not Lance's first choice as a career. An engineer by training (he read Engineering Science at Oxford), he had set his heart on a job in management in British manufacturing.

If you believe what you read in the newspapers, British industry is crying out for people like Lance. But if Lance's experience is anything to go by, this simply isn't true. British industry may complain that the brightest and the best scorn industry for the quick fix of the City, but Lance tells a different story: 'While I was at Harvard, I wrote to nine of Britain's biggest engineering companies, enquiring about jobs. Only three bothered to reply and they all said there were no opportunities for someone with my training.'

Between Oxford and Harvard, Lance spent two and a half years in the London office of management consultants Bain and Company. Lance left Grosvenor at the end of 1992. He has returned to consultancy, this time with the Cambridge-based Scientific Generics, which advises technology companies. At Grosvenor, Lance found that he wanted to continue working closely with the companies in which he invested. But as a venture capitalist this isn't possible. Venture capitalists get involved in strategic decisions, but they tend to stay away from the day-to-day management of the companies in which they invest. At Scientific Generics Lance hopes to be able to get involved in management at an operational as well as strategic level.

Trevor Bayley, an economics graduate from Cambridge, is 31 and although he left Grosvenor at the end of August 1992 he was involved with some important deals during the time the television cameras were tracking events. Trained as an accountant, Trevor joined Grosvenor from the industrial company, Morgan Crucible, where he was responsible for evaluating and negotiating acquisitions. Like Lance, Trevor was also frustrated that as a venture capitalist he was not able to have much say in the management of the companies in which he invested. He commented that, 'As venture capitalists go, Grosvenor takes a very hands-on* approach to its investments. But in reality there is a limit to what you can do if you are only visiting the company once a month and all you see is board minutes.'

Trevor has gone to work for Tiphook, an entrepreneurial leasing company, where he is working as a kind of internal firefighter stepping in and solving specific management problems. At Grosvenor he learnt how important it is for companies to think strategically. At his new job Trevor experiences the day-to-day problems of management. He simply has to roll his sleeves up and get stuck in at a level where, hopefully, he will be able to have a direct and almost immediate impact on profits.

Stephen Edwards is Grosvenor's newest executive and is aged 28. With his striped shirts and braces, he is the only Grosvenor executive who wouldn't look out of place in the City. A qualified accountant with Coopers & Lybrand, he specialized in corporate finance and, in particular, advising management teams in larger venture capital transactions. His 18-month secondment to Grosvenor was an obvious way to experience the world of venture capital from the inside and to extend his experience to smaller transactions. He has now decided to join Grosvenor full time.

As Robert Drummond admits, it is seldom possible to assess how a new recruit to venture capital will turn out. To be good, you need to be able to juggle several balls at once, argue convincingly with management teams, and be stubborn enough to argue your case. Grosvenor was disappointed at losing two junior members of its team in 1992, but Julian Carr strengthened the team again late in the year. He is an experienced young accountant who spent two years with the captive venture capital company County NatWest Ventures. Julian says he was keen to join a smaller outfit that gave him more latitude to develop his skills and to take on increased responsibilities.

Chapter Three

The London Arena

The London Arena, the concert and exhibition hall in London's
Docklands, is inextricably linked with Frank Warren, the boxing
promoter who was dramatically gunned down in November 1990
as he left a dinner at the Broadway Theatre in Barking. The sen-
sational arrest of former world champion boxer, Terry Marsh – the
fighting fireman – for attempted murder, his subsequent trial and
acquittal meant that for a while the two were hardly out of the
headlines.

The London Arena was Frank Warren's baby. It was his dream
to create a concert and exhibition hall to rival Wembley in
the heart of the new emerging Docklands. As executive chairman, he was actively involved in the day-to-day management
of the place and he has always claimed that the shooting,
his convalescence and the subsequent trial contributed to the
Arena's problems. Six months later in May 1991, the American
bank Security Pacific, which had invested £30 million into the
place, called in the receiver and Frank Warren threw in the
towel.

The London Arena is a big grey and blue metal-clad box on the
Isle of Dogs, in the heart of the new Docklands. It's a huge versatile
space which can be used for any number of events such as pop
concerts, sporting events, conferences, new product launches and
exhibitions.

It's basically a bums on seats business. The more events which
are attracted to the Arena, the greater the rental income. The more
people who come through the doors, the greater the number of

drinks, hamburgers, pizzas, T-shirts and baseball hats that can be sold to them.

If the pop promoters and exhibition and conference organizers could be persuaded to use it; if visitors could be persuaded that Docklands was not some inaccessible no man's land, and if the costs could be got under control, then the London Arena was a potential goldmine. But these were big ifs.

Mel Hague and Mandy Rayner were trying to raise the finance to buy the business from the receiver. Mel Hague had been involved with the Arena since it was no more than a rusty banana warehouse. He was a director of the company which had owned it, although in the Frank Warren days he was not concerned with its day-to-day management. Having helped get the project off the ground in the early 1980s when the development of Docklands was only just beginning, he had a tremendous emotional attachment to the project.

Mandy Rayner was the Arena's first employee when it opened in 1989, and rose to become company secretary. Armed with business plans* and cash flow forecasts could they persuade someone to back them in a project which was going to cost many millions of pounds to get off the ground? They had taken the first steps towards strengthening their management team with the recruitment of a new sales and marketing man, Rod Gunner, from the Robert Stigwood group, the pop concert promoters.

Mel Hague and Mandy Rayner's advisers from accountants Stoy Hayward had put them in touch with Grosvenor who had given Janis Anderson the job of seeing whether or not there was a deal to be done. Her manner is relaxed, but she has a persistence, a doggedness which doesn't allow her to give up on problems until she has explored them from every conceivable angle.

Here was a deal which showed just how creative and flexible venture capitalists often need to be to get a company, or the people who are to run it, into the kind of shape where it is worth backing. This was an unusual deal for Grosvenor, one which Janis described as effectively a start up.

It was certainly a deal with many twists and turns. It began with the search for a new executive chairman to strengthen the management team. The team then made an offer to the receiver which was based in part on the Arena's future performance. When this was turned down Janis decided to make the offer more attractive to the receiver by improving the management rather than by increasing the offer. She managed to find a potential new managing director, but her hopes of strengthening the management team were dashed when the first management team decided to look elsewhere for finance, and the new managing director decided she wasn't the right person for the job.

Finally she explored the possibility of a joint venture with an Irish venue operator. And while Janis struggled to get the management team right she never knew whether or not the receiver and Security Pacific would be prepared to accept her offer.

Janis lived with this deal for four and a half long months; four and a half months in which she got married, honeymooned and was made a director of Grosvenor Venture Managers. It was always a risky deal but one which Janis believed had enormous potential. In the end Janis failed because her offer wasn't high enough but she also failed because she couldn't persuade all her colleagues at Grosvenor, and the non-executive directors of Grosvenor's three unquoted funds, that this was a deal worth backing.

However, it does demonstrate Janis's ability to grapple with complex and intricate deals. Grosvenor intended leading the deal with Lloyds Development Capital, the venture capital arm of Lloyds Bank. In terms of financial commitment the deal was significant but it didn't rank among Grosvenor's largest deals and the two venture capitalists always intended finding a third partner once the deal was concluded.

The original offer was £4 million up front with up to £6 million in eight years, the final amount to be determined by the Arena's performance. If the bookings didn't materialize the venture capitalists would probably lose all their money. On the other hand if the Arena lived up to, or exceeded, its forecasts, they would have had a big share in a company which was immensely profitable. There was also the added bonus of some surplus land on the site which would have development potential once the depressed Docklands property market picked up.

In October 1991, at the preliminary stage, Janis only had a rough idea of what went wrong at the Arena. She knew the bookings started to drop off, that there was trouble keeping the overheads under control and not enough money was spent on marketing. She had also heard complaints about the organization of the place. However, she had also been told that the place got off to a good start when it opened in 1989 with 95 bookings in the first year, including the highly successful launch of the new Ford Fiesta, and that bookings were even higher in the second year.

One of her first concerns centred on the quality of the management team which had assembled the bid for the Arena. She was not sure she or her colleagues would support a management team associated with the company's collapse. And she was already thinking actively about finding a strong executive chairman to strengthen the management team.

Friday, 18 October 1991

Janis needed to know what potential users of the Arena thought about the place. She arranged a meeting with Terry Neill, the former Northern Ireland football international and manager, now in the promotions industry. According to him the major obstacle to bookings was the problem of access. Promoters wouldn't use the Arena because there was a fear that events would flop because Docklands was so difficult to get to. He confirmed Janis's feeling that the building itself was held in high regard, but he thought it might be ten years before Dockland's infrastructure problems were resolved.

The Arena management team had addressed the problem of access in their business plan. According to Mel Hague, access to the Arena was not a problem. They said it was more a question of *persuading* the public that Docklands was not more difficult to get to than Wembley. They pointed to the new transport links which were being built over the next two and half years which should further improve access.

Access to the Arena was one of Janis's major worries. She had still not made up her mind whether the problem was real or just one of public perception as the management team claimed.

Thursday, 24 October 1991.

At the regular weekly progress meeting at Grosvenor Janis brought the good news that she had also found a potential executive chairman for the Arena.

Wednesday, 30 October 1991.

Janis took the Docklands Light Railway to Crossharbour, the stop on the line which dropped her directly in front of the Arena. Janis had never encountered any problems getting there which made her veer towards the view that the access problem was more one of public perception than structural inadequacies.

She was there for a meeting with Mel Hague, Mandy Rayner and Rod Gunner and to have another look round the building. The witches and wizards from the previous night's Halloween Smash Hits Poll Award Winners party had abandoned their lurid green cauldrons and dayglo orange pumpkins. There were now only two further bookings. After the end of November there was nothing and the receiver wouldn't be taking any more bookings until the Arena's future was decided.

The management team had already put in a bid to the receiver and they were understandably anxious for a reply. Rod Gunner was particularly impatient. He felt that unless they seized the initiative, the receiver might be tempted to hold on to their bid in the hope that something better would come along. For example, it was well known in the trade that Wembley were interested in launching a bid. However, the receiver couldn't act without the approval of Security Pacific the major creditor. The bank was meant to be sending somebody over from the States to deal with the problem, but he had been delayed for three weeks. It was agreed to ask the management team's adviser from Stoy Hayward to put pressure on the receiver for a quick decision.

Janis was still gnawing away at the problem of access. Rod Gunner was convinced that it was not a problem. According to him, nothing stops people going to see a good band and bands which can fill the Arena's 12 500 seats were by definition in this category. Mel was sure that the Docklands' current television advertising campaign would help people conquer their irrational fear of the area. He catalogued the planned transport improvements: a second tunnel on the Docklands Light Railway was to open later in the year which would improve the railway's connection to Bank tube station making it much easier for passengers to transfer on to the railway rather than having to make the trek from Tower Hill station to the railway station at Tower Gateway. The eventual installation of a new computer would also mean an end to the delays and breakdowns for which the railway was infamous. And with each train capable of taking between 400 and 440 passengers, it would only take 15 trains to fill half the Arena.

32

New roads, including the Limehouse Link, being built by the London Docklands Development Corporation, the final stages of which were due to open in the spring of 1993, would improve access to Docklands making it much easier to get both into London and out on to the M11 and M25. London City Airport had recently been upgraded and, according to Rod Gunner, at one recent exhibition one in ten exhibitors came in through the airport.

This was the honeymoon stage which every deal goes through if it gets beyond the just dating stage. Janis was optimistic. She said: 'If I can find the right chairman to introduce to the management team and if the negotiated price stays around where it is at the moment, I feel that this deal could be done.'

Mandy Rayner, who was clearly unaware that Janis's calm, unflappable exterior cleverly concealed much frantic underwater paddling was dewey eyed in her praise: 'She has become almost a friend; she is helping me with my dream.'

Monday, 4 November 1991.

Janis brought Michael Glover, the Grosvenor director in overall charge of the deal, up to date. Security Pacific had turned down the management team's offer of £4 million up front with another £6 million in eight years' time secured on the property. Security Pacific had made it clear that it was reluctant to do a deferred payment deal with a management team so closely linked with the previous management. Janis was unwilling to pay more, so she decided to see if she could make the offer more attractive to the bank by strengthening the management team with a new managing director.

Janis had already broached Mel on the subject of bringing in a new managing director. It would mean Mel stepping down and finding some other role for himself within the organization. Much to Janis's surprise, Mel had agreed to think about it.

Janis had also spotted another fly in the ointment. She didn't think there was a serious counter bid from Wembley in the pipeline. However, she did think that Security Pacific could decide to put in its own temporary management team and sit tight until the economy and Docklands picked itself up when they could hope to get a better price.

Up until now Janis had been working alone on the Arena. However, later in the week Janis was in contact with Anthea Harrison of Lloyds Development Capital and they agreed to start working together on the Arena as joint deal leaders. Quite by chance Anthea knew someone who might be interested in the job of managing director.

Thursday, 7 November, 1991.
Mel Hague was unhappy with Grosvenor's attempts to strengthen the management. He had decided he would like to remain as managing director and he telephoned Janis to tell her he now wanted to look for other sources of venture capital who might be prepared to pay more than Grosvenor for the Arena.

Thursday, 21 November 1991.
Janis and Anthea Harrison from Lloyds Development Capital had arranged a meeting with Security Pacific to find out if there was a basis on which they could do a deal. Janis left the meeting with her hopes raised. The bank had several options. She had been told that Wembley and Irish venue organizers, Apollo, were interested but only if they could lease the Arena. In other words they weren't interested in buying it. The bank could put its own management in, or they could sell it. Janis was convinced the bank would prefer to sell it.

The last booking, a pop concert for the group Skid Row – billed all over London as 'too wild for Wembley' – was the following day, and Security Pacific wanted to make a decision one way or the other within the next two to three weeks. Janis was now under enormous pressure. She had very little time to finalize her management team and organize accountants' and surveyors' reports.

Wednesday, 27 November 1991.

Janis's hopes of putting together a new management team were dashed when the person she had lined up as the potential new managing director pulled out. She telephoned Anthea at Lloyds Development Capital to share the bad news. She was disappointed but philosophical: 'It was worth a try. Every now and then these things work and probably nine times out of ten they don't.'

She put the telephone down and went straight into the weekly work-in-progress meeting. The potential new managing director had decided not to take the job because she felt she lacked the contacts in the pop concert industry which would really be needed to drive the company ahead in its first months. Janis didn't want to spend any more time on the deal if it meant assembling another management team and it was agreed that the cost of a headhunter couldn't be justified.

Even so Janis left the door ajar. The receiver and bank now knew that Grosvenor was interested in financing the Arena, and she was sure that they would put any interested operators in touch with them. But for the moment at least, Janis had closed the file on Arena.

But it didn't stay closed for long. It appeared that the theatre operators, Apollo Leisure, had been talking to the receiver. Apollo is the biggest theatre operator in Europe including the Apollo Victoria – the London home of 'Starlight Express' – the Liverpool Empire and Bristol Hippodrome. It had experience of running a multi-purpose arena at The Point in Dublin which has 8000 seats and runs along similar lines to the London and Wembley arenas.

Apollo didn't have the resources to buy the Arena on its own, but instead of simply leasing it, Apollo was interested in doing a joint venture with someone like Grosvenor. The receiver had put

Apollo in touch with Grosvenor and Lloyds Development Capital to see if they could work out a deal to buy the Arena.

The big worry with joint venture deals like this is how does the venture capitalist get out at a fair price when one of the joint venture partners is actually managing the business and would normally have first refusal on the shares.

Monday, 6 January 1992.

The team from Apollo had now prepared sales and profit forecasts for the Arena. With Janis on her honeymoon the Apollo team, managing director, David Rogers, operations director, Sam Shrouder, and Mike Adamson had arrived at Grosvenor's offices for a meeting with Anthea Harrison from Lloyds Development Capital and Trevor Bayley from Grosvenor.

Apollo was working on the assumption that Security Pacific would accept a deal which gave them cash up front of £3 million and a deferred element of £5 million. The team expected to have bookings for 50 days in the first year and around 66 in the second year. They intended concentrating on pop concerts to begin with. Exhibitions are booked a couple of years in advance so it would be some time before they would once again be seen at the Arena. The licence restricted the Arena to 120 days of bookings a year, a figure which Apollo didn't expect to be approaching until the fifth year.

Sam Shrouder claimed they had deliberately played down the number of bookings which they thought they could achieve. Even on this conservative basis, the potential for making money out of the Arena looked promising. On these projections, Apollo reckoned the Arena could break even in the first year, with profits of £360 000 in the second year, rising to £1.6 million plus in the fifth year.

Grosvenor were treating this as an entirely new deal and it was now working from information provided entirely by Apollo. In a previous meeting, Grosvenor's Michael Glover described year one as the white knuckle ride. With the exception of bands with an overnight success on their hands, most concerts are booked at least six months ahead, so there was going to be a time lag of between four and six months before the first bookings took place and the Arena started earning any revenue.

It was to be a joint venture with a third each owned by Grosvenor, Lloyds Development Capital and Apollo. The new company would then negotiate a separate contract with Apollo to manage the Arena. Apollo had earmarked one of its employees to manage the Arena, although to get the full benefit of Apollo's marketing expertise and sales contracts, the bookings would be made centrally from the company's Oxford headquarters.

There would be other benefits of scale too. For example, Apollo's purchasing muscle would mean significantly higher profits for the restaurants and bars.

36

Anthea Harrison from Lloyds Development Capital raised the problem of how to structure the deal in a way which allowed the venture capitalists to get their money out at a fair price. David Rogers said Janis had previously mentioned that Grosvenor would like to have a formula written into the arrangement for determining the price at which the venture capitalist would require Apollo to buy their shares. David said he couldn't accept that. He reminded everyone that Apollo was no stranger to joint ventures. It had partners in several concert venues including The Point, in Dublin.

He wanted a deal which gave him first refusal on the shares when the venture capitalist wanted to sell out but he wanted to be able to negotiate the price at the time. The problem for venture capitalists in this sort of deal is that there is a potential conflict of interest between the outside investors – in this case Grosvenor and Lloyds Development Capital – and the managers – in this case Apollo – with the outside investors never quite sure whether or not the managers are depressing performance so that they can eventually buy out the outside investors on the cheap.

It was agreed that this aspect of the deal needed a great deal more work. The question of the exit* mechanism was going to make it hard for Anthea Harrison to sell the deal to her board. As she said to Apollo, 'You and I can never be quite on the same side of the table.' And when venture capitalists are so keen on the idea of partnership with investors and managers all pulling in the same direction, it has the potential for turning into a somewhat uneasy alliance.

Thursday, 9 January 1992.
In Janis's absence Trevor brought the regular Grosvenor Thursday morning work-in-progress meeting up to date on the Arena deal. He had been concerned about whether Grosvenor could get locked into this investment when the only effective buyer was Apollo. Robert Drummond was slightly more sanguine. The project had healthy asset backing and so long as Apollo was putting in a sizeable amount of money and didn't have a controlling stake, he was reasonably happy.

Thursday, 16 January 1992.
Janis was back from her honeymoon, looking tanned and relaxed. The London Arena was now rather more than a spectoral presence at the Thursday morning progress meetings. Robert Drummond and Michael Glover, who had discussed it informally during the week, although basically keen on the deal, still had one or two reservations.

Michael was concerned that Apollo intended turning the London Arena into just another pop concert venue and that they had no intention or management ability to exploit its potential as an exhibition centre. If that was the case Grosvenor had to be clear in its own mind that that was what it was backing.

Janis explained that pop concerts were where the highest margins were to be found and Trevor was convinced that there was a vast unmet demand in London for pop concert venues of the size of the London and Wembley Arenas. Michael wanted to see evidence that the market was there and Apollo wasn't just out to steal Wembley's market share which would provoke retaliatory action.

Since she had just returned from holiday, Janis hadn't got the facts and figures at her finger tips. She promised an analysis of the market plus a close comparison of how Wembley and the London Arena compared for the next meeting. Janis now knew she had a battle on her hands if she was to persuade her colleagues that she hadn't been wasting the last four months and that the London Arena had enormous potential to make money for Grosvenor.

Thursday, 23 January 1992.
The regular Thursday progress meeting came round again and doubts were still being expressed on the wisdom of the Arena deal. This time it was Bill Edge who was unhappy when he finally realized that Grosvenor got absolutely no security because the level of bank borrowings needed to finance the deal and provide the working capital were likely to exceed the value of the building. Michael and Robert on the other hand were enthusiastic. Michael was clearly impressed by Apollo's track record. Robert pointed out that in most deals the management team demanded preferential terms, but here the venture capitalists and the management were going in as equal partners. 'This is not that risky a deal unless you believe the Arena is a total white elephant,' was Robert's comment as he wound up the meeting.

Wednesday, 19 February 1992.
The London Arena was to go to Grosvenor's investment committee today and Janis had to summon all her powers of persuasion to convince her colleagues that the London Arena would make a lot of money for Grosvenor and that the effort she had put into matching up Apollo with the Arena hadn't been wasted.

Janis would emphasize the positive aspects of the deal, the link with Apollo, and play down the negative aspects, such as the poor transport links to Docklands. She wanted the investment committee, which compromised Robert Drummond, Michael Glover, Bill Edge and Tony Crook, to concentrate on Apollo's expertise and proven track record in managing entertainment venues up and down the country and in Ireland rather than on the shortcomings of the Arena itself. It is Apollo's ability to do package deals with pop groups, offering a number of different concert halls throughout the country to which the Arena could be added which Janis was convinced made this deal so attractive.

Bill Edge quickly said he didn't feel that this was an investment he could support. He simply didn't believe that the Arena could be run at a profit when the previous management were only managing to fill it for 70 days a year and he estimated that it needed 83 days' worth of bookings before the place broke even.

The meeting was not going at all well for Janis. Only Robert and Michael supported it. Robert took the view that if the thing worked there was considerable potential for making a lot of money. He suggested a compromise: Grosvenor would limit its investment to £1 million, the deal would go no further unless Janis could line up another venture capital partner before rather than after the deal was done, and the final decision should rest with the boards of the Grosvenor funds.

Janis might have been upset but she regained her composure remarkably quickly. She brought herself back down to earth when she reminded herself that whatever Grosvenor decided, there was no deal at all unless Security Pacific agreed to play ball and sell the Arena to them.

Wednesday, 25 February 1992.

This was Janis's last chance to keep the Arena deal alive. Yesterday, she had heard that Security Pacific had turned down the offer with Apollo, although she thought they were still open to negotiation. Having failed to win over all her colleagues, she now had to persuade the non-executive directors of the Grosvenor funds to back her judgement. Without their approval there would be no point in pursuing the deal with the bank any further. The three unquoted funds shared substantially the same directors and held board meetings concurrently before the board meeting of the quoted investment trust, Grosvenor Development Capital (GDC). So Janis had to face first the unquoted funds' boards and, secondly, that of GDC.

But there was also the question of the Arena's licence. This had recently been renewed by the receiver who wasn't in a strong enough position to oppose the additional restrictions placed on it. If Grosvenor gave the deal the amber light, Apollo would appeal against the licence at a hearing which had been set for 12 March, and if they didn't get the changes they wanted, the deal was off anyway. If Grosvenor turned the deal down at this meeting, Apollo wouldn't be in any position to appeal, so there would be no chance of reviving the deal later.

The fact that this deal had come to the board with no clear recommendation from the investment committee was hardly a glowing start.

Chairman John Oakley and a number of the other non-executive directors voiced a whole array of objections most of which Janis had hoped she had covered in her committee paper. The lack of transport, the licence, the ability to fill the Arena, the extent of the previous management's losses, were all raised adding to the general feeling that here was a deal as risky as the riskiest start-up.

Robert gave the deal his unequivocal support. At one point he said:

'Property is as cheap as it will ever be. I believe this is an opportunist deal. I believe that we have in Apollo probably the only people that could actually do it. That doesn't necessarily mean that it will be successful but I think we have got about the best package we could have at the lowest point in time. I think it is worth doing.'

But he was not prepared to go to the stake for it. John Oakley was strongly of the opinion that they should have nothing to do with it. At the suggestion that Janis should go away and do more work, Robert was adamant that Janis shouldn't commit much more time to the deal and that they should either kill the deal or do it.

Up until now Janis had given no indication of just how important the deal was to her. It had been four and a half long months of hard sweat. There were the original negotiations with the first management team, the search for new managers, talks with Apollo and the structuring of an unusual joint venture deal. Just for a split second a look of anger, irritation and disappointment crossed her face.

It was decided to leave the deal on the table just in case Apollo was able to confirm any of the 28 provisional bookings which the Arena's receiver had lined up. But Janis knew in her heart that the deal was dead. As she said:

'Venture capitalism is not about one person going off and doing their own thing. At the end of the day, if you can't persuade your colleagues, then you don't do the deal. One day out of five you go home pissed off with something. That's the nature of the business. You have to go on to the next deal. But if you have put a lot of work in to something, it is personally very disappointing. There is always a way to do a deal. In this case I didn't find it partly because we weren't going to be forced to pay more than we thought it was worth.'

In a cruel twist of fate later that day, the quoted investment trust, GDC, agreed to put money into the Arena. But it was too late. Without the support of the other funds, GDC didn't have sufficient resources to back the Arena on its own, so the deal was still as good as dead.

In February 1993, the Arena was being used by pop groups as a rehearsal room and Security Pacific and the receiver were in discussions with an operator who had expressed an interest in running the place. Apollo subsequently bought the Odeon Hammersmith, now renamed the Apollo Hammersmith, which gives the company a major London concert venue.

Chapter Four

Watershed

Grant Bovey at 31 is a young man with just about everything going for him. He has lashings of charm, an easy going manner and the film star looks of a young Robert Redford; all qualities destined to raise instant alarm bells with any venture capitalist worth his salt.

His company, Watershed Pictures, produces videos for sale rather than rental. The company has carved itself a lucrative niche producing motor racing videos with Nigel Mansell but it also produces football, comedy and children's programmes as well.

Grant Bovey came to Grosvenor to raise the additional working capital which he would need if he was to continue developing his company. He was in some hurry to conclude a deal. Watershed was facing a severe cash flow squeeze brought about by the company's rapid expansion – a squeeze exacerbated by the seasonal nature of the business, with sales reaching their peak in the Christmas period – and it also had an inadequate overdraft facility.

Grant has spent most of his working life in the video industry. He learnt his craft with a company called Braveworld which, when Grant worked there, was involved with acquiring the UK video rights to films which it distributed through the video rental market. At Braveworld he worked his way up to the position of sales director before striking out on his own with Watershed Pictures.

Watershed is still a very young company as Grant Bovey explained: 'The company was formed at the end of 1988. The main purpose was to acquire film rights for the United Kingdom at a time when the video rental market was very buoyant indeed.'

However, after six months Grant knew that the main opportunity was not in the video rental market which had begun to stagnate almost as quickly as it had boomed, but in producing videos for sale, what the trade calls the 'sell-through' market. In 1989 the video rental market peaked with the public spending £569 million on renting videos. By 1991 this figure had fallen to £544 million and there was a further fall to £511 million in 1992. On the other hand sales of videos were still growing in spite of the recession with sales of £300 million in 1989 growing to £375 million by 1991, and a further increase to £400 million forecast in 1992.

Instead of struggling along, Watershed saw the way the wind was blowing. Grant says:

'In the middle of 1989 a decision was taken that we should become seriously involved in the video 'sell-through' market. But whereas most companies would sit behind their desks and wait for the telephone to ring and for people to offer them programmes, we didn't want to rely on other people and we decided to generate our own programmes. We wanted to rely on our own creativity rather than other people's.'

With its football and motor racing videos Watershed has helped solve the problem of what to give dad for Christmas, so much so that the vast majority – around 65 per cent – of Watershed's video sales take place in the last three months of the year in the run up to Christmas.

Apart from the cash flow problems which this presented, the actual number of new videos which Watershed was producing was growing fast. In 1990 the company produced just 22 videos, in 1991 the number had increased to 42 and there was a move into television production with a five-part television series on motor racing for Japanese television. In 1992 the company produced 75 hours of output, including 18 one-hour motor racing programmes for Japanese television.

In Watershed's early years, costs were both easy to predict and easy to contain. For example, *Classic Morecambe and Wise* – a series which now runs to six volumes – is a selection of some of the comedians' best known sketches put together with the addition of a new introduction from Ernie Wise reminiscing about the old days. Before buying the film footage from the BBC, Watershed signed a distribution deal for the proposed video with one of the big video distributors who sell the videos to the high street retailers.

Watershed's first distribution deal with Virgin Vision gave the company an advance of £250 000 on 16 proposed video productions. With this sort of deal Watershed was able to predict its income and if sales rose above the agreed level any extra income was the icing on the cake.

Watershed has been particularly successful with its football and motor racing videos. Grant developed a close working friendship with the 1992 world motor racing champion, Nigel Mansell, Britain's greatest formula one driver since Jackie Stewart, and this resulted in a number of top selling motor racing videos featuring Mansell.

But the video market is becoming more and more cut throat and the stakes are getting higher. Sporting bodies are selling exclusive video rights in the same way they sell television rights. And with a growing number of companies pitching for these video contracts the price is going up all the time.

In January 1991, Watershed entered into a £600 000 five-year video and television rights deal with the Football Association. Winning this exclusive rights deal with the Football Association was a great achievement for Watershed, which was still a very small company, and it was a real feather in Grant's cap. He won the contract against strong competition, not because he offered more than anyone else but because he showed a certain nerve in putting in an offer which wasn't all hedged around with conditions. It was this deal which forced Grant Bovey to look for new sources of finance and to consider the possibility of venture capital.

Watershed's other great asset was Nigel Mansell. Grant was taking a big risk when he signed up Nigel Mansell for the first two videos. Grant's faith in Nigel Mansell paid off and there is no doubt that the name Nigel Mansell on the video wrapper has enormous pulling power with the public.

When Grosvenor first became involved with Watershed, the Company had already made four Mansell videos and another five were planned for 1992. When the fifth Mansell video came out in the last week of November 1991, it sold 50 000 copies in its first four weeks. A similar tape, but without the Mansell magic ingredient, released by the Formula One governing body, FOCA, sold significantly less well.

Developments in the football world, such as the Premier League and the 1994 World Cup in the United States, looked set to provide Watershed with plenty of opportunities for expanding its output. And Grant Bovey was very optimistic about the future.

But it was equally clear that he needed additional finance if the company was to carry on growing. Grant Bovey considered all the options, including an offer for the company from the independent television producer, Sunset & Vine, as he said:

'Borrowing money from the bank is not possible because they don't understand our kind of business. Our assets are not tied up in bricks and mortar; they are tied up in our debtors – the people who owe us money – and the investment we make in our programmes including copyrights which are extremely difficult to put a value on. There are no tangible assets to speak of which makes the banks nervous. Normally they only feel happy if they know there are assets which can be sold if the business goes bust.

'I have had offers to buy the company, but after talking to my colleagues in Watershed we all feel the company still had a lot more potential and if we sold out now, we could be kicking ourselves in a couple of years' time.

'Venture capital was the other possibility. Some people refer to venture capitalists as vultures, but I think they are an essential part of the business community because they are providing me with a service which suits me. They give me the necessary funds to progress the business over the next six to nine months and, if things go well, I retain control of my company and if propositions and deals come to me in the next 12 months I can go back to them and say, "Hey guys, we need another half a million pounds to do this," and the chances are they will do it.'

Two months later, having been through the venture capital wringer, Grant Bovey no longer had such a romantic view of venture capital. In October they were the knights in shining armour; by December all such illusions were smashed. In October we saw a confident, cheerful, young man with an irresistible urge to build his business and build it fast. In December Grant was tired, exhausted and somewhat chastened by his experience, but it didn't feel as if it would be too long before his old ebullient self made a comeback.

The deal came to Grosvenor via the merchant bank, Rea Brothers, which had been advising Grant.

Monday, 7 October 1991.

By this time, senior Grosvenor director, Tony Crook, and new executive, Lance Phillips, had spent the last three weeks looking at Watershed, how it operated, how the finances worked and the market in which it competes. It was now time to persuade Grosvenor's investment committee that this one was worth a more detailed look.

This was Lance's first big deal at Grosvenor. And, at 27, he was not that much younger than Grant. Lance had done most of the spade work, preparing the report for the investment committee and designing the structure of the deal. For Lance a lot hung on this deal. He was convinced that Watershed was a worthwhile investment, although he did have his fears as he explained:

'The people at Watershed have an infectious energy, enthusiasm and commitment to their business and I think they have a lot of ability too. Having said that, this being my first deal, it's very nerve wracking to have a business which is built round one person. Grant's ability is undoubtedly vital. For my first deal it would have been nice to have had a company with a lot of asset backing just in case there is a downslide and the deal doesn't go terribly well.'

If he managed to do the deal on favourable terms and the investment went well, he would make a good impression on his new employers. In the venture capital business you are only as good as your last deal and for Lance getting off on the right foot was essential if he was to persuade the powers that be at Grosvenor that he had the makings of a venture capitalist.

With so much at stake it is hardly surprising that Lance was nervous as he waited to be called into the investment committee meeting. He didn't really know what to expect. Lance was extremely enthusiastic about Watershed, but it was a risky deal and he wanted the committee to see the company for what it was, warts and all. Lance saw it as an intellectual problem, taking the view that here was a gathering of intelligent people which wanted to make a rational decision. He wanted the committee to see the negative as well as the positive; to understand clearly how he had reached the conclusion that Watershed was an investment worth backing.

He didn't expect to have to sell the deal and he was surprised when he realized that this was what the investment committee was expecting him to do.

When you have been living a deal day and night for three weeks it begins to be difficult to see the wood for the trees. It is then up to the investment committee to ask the fundamental questions. What Robert Drummond wanted to know was why Watershed needed any money at all when most of the stock was presold to distribution companies.

Other executives might have taken this as their cue to ram home the key message that Watershed needed the money to pay for valuable exclusive video rights to various sporting events, such as the five-year exclusive video rights with the FA.

Instead Lance launched into a discussion of Watershed's cash flow problems over the Christmas period. The money from Watershed's all-important Christmas sales doesn't arrive in the company's bank account until the following February or March.

However, by taking the investment committee through one of the more negative aspects of this potential investment, Lance gave them the chance to look at Watershed's relationship with its bank. Watershed used to share the same bank as Castle Communications, the company which gave Watershed a helping hand in its early days and which took a quarter stake in December 1989. Castle Communications had recently moved its account to a new bank, which in turn seemed to have affected Watershed's relationship with its bank where the overdraft limit was frozen at £100 000 a figure which the company had, by this time outgrown. But as Robert pointed out, the gaps left by unimaginative bankers were there to be plugged by the venture capitalists.

There are many different organizations and financial transactions involved with each video, especially sports videos, where there may be an exclusive video rights deal with a sporting organization, another deal to buy the actual film footage from the BBC or ITV, and then yet another with a video distributor. Robert Drummond was keen to get it clear in his own mind who paid what to whom and when, and whether or not profits could be squeezed by competition entering the market or someone in the chain abusing their monopoly position and suddenly upping the ante.

Lance's explanation seemed to satisfy Robert that these multilayered video deals were an example of mutual back scratching and in everyone's interest. The sport concerned got additional funds while the TV companies got a useful additional source of revenue – most have more film and video footage than they could ever turn out on their own label. It was Lance's view that the only weak link was the distributor. Watershed was now large enough to think about cutting out the distributor. These days three-quarters of all videos are sold through just six large high street chains, and Watershed had discussed hiring a couple of salesmen and dispensing with the services of a distributor.

Grant Bovey's youth and lack of management experience were factors which Lance had skated over in his report. 'How old is Grant Bovey?' was the question he was dreading. But when it finally came it produced less comment than he expected; somehow the committee was not surprised by the revelation that Grant was only 31.

Lance relaxed, but he was somewhat taken aback by the vehemence of Bill Edge's concerns over the balance sheet. Bill was worried by the high level of stocks and wanted to know how they were valued because if they were overvalued then the company's apparently healthy profits would be nothing but an illusion.

As Bill pointed out a company like Watershed, where stock is an important item on the balance sheet, can produce wildly different trading results depending on how the stock is valued. If production costs are written off over a long period then the stock value will be high and profits will be correspondingly inflated. If on the other hand production costs are written off over a shorter period then the stock value is lower and profits will be more modest. Everyone had in mind the previous year's collapse of video distributor, Parkfield, which went bust owing many hundreds of millions of pounds because it overestimated the size of the video market and was left with warehouses full of near worthless stock.

Lance explained that production costs are written off over three years with half written off in the first year and that as this is a much shorter period than most other video companies there is no danger of Watershed's profits being overstated. (Later, Watershed decided to write their production costs off over the even shorter period of two years.) So the decision was made to send in a firm of accountants to check on the accounting policies and the effect these might have on Watershed's profits. The suggestion was also made that Watershed ought to think of changing its accountant to a larger firm and that some thought should be given as to whether or not this should be a condition of doing the deal.

Lance was now almost certain the deal would be given the go ahead. He suggested a structure which allowed for the fact that in October – when this meeting was taking place – Watershed couldn't predict how many videos it was going to sell in the run up to Christmas. However, Watershed expected to make pre-tax profits of £800 000 if sales over the Christmas period went as well as expected, but Lance couldn't be sure that the company would achieve this.

To allow for the risk that Watershed might not achieve its profit target, Lance built a ratchet* into the deal which linked the price Grosvenor paid for its shares to Watershed's eventual profits.

The offer which Watershed received from the independent television production company, Sunset & Vine, was based on the company's historic profits, so a deal which took into account

Watershed's phenomenal growth over the previous year might well persuade Grant Bovey to go with Grosvenor rather than Sunset & Vine.

Robert Drummond suggested it would be a good idea for Grosvenor to buy Castle's stake in Watershed before doing the deal with Grant. However, he conceded that it might not be possible and agreed not to make it a condition of doing the deal.

Lance had been selling the concept of a partnership to Grant who wanted to feel free to come back to Grosvenor for additional finance, especially if he landed a big exclusive rights deal. Lance suggested that this could be done with a high yielding preference share which could be convertible into ordinary shares. The meeting was all but over and so the idea of the share became just another detail to be resolved later.

The speed with which the meeting finally made up its mind took Lance aback. The deal got the go ahead subject to an accountant's report. It was agreed that Tony Crook should go on the board as a non-executive director. And negotiations to acquire Castle Communications' share in Watershed were to start immediately.

Lance emerged from the meeting visibly jubilant. At that moment he would really have liked to share the good news with Grant Bovey. He and Grant had both learned a lot about venture capital over the last month. He headed for the phone but Grant was out and the call was taken at Watershed by Kim Clayton, the company's financial director, and Grant's right hand woman. She was thrilled, but it was all a bit of an anti-climax, especially as he had been nursing a secret ambition that the investment committee might put his name forward as the Grosvenor non-executive director of Watershed.

This should have been the end of Lance's worries. In fact, the Watershed deal with Grosvenor was far from being sewn up. News of Grosvenor's decision to back Watershed travelled fast. It stirred Baronsmead, a venture capital operation with close links to Barclays Bank, Watershed's bank, into action. Grant got a call from Baronsmead. As he said: 'I felt like the girl who hasn't had a date for a while who as soon as she starts going out with someone, suddenly finds herself inundated with offers.'

Wednesday, 16 October 1991.

It was the week before the Japanese Grand Prix and Grant Bovey was due to fly out to Japan. He was hoping to land a big and very profitable television deal on motor racing with Japanese Satellite Broadcasting and he was milking his connections with Nigel Mansell for all they were worth. Dinner with Nigel Mansell could be the bait which clinched the deal.

When the dust settled later Lance was able to recognize that Grant Bovey's cool handling of his two suitors was a true demonstration of his ability as an entrepreneur, the very skills venture capitalists are so desperate to find and develop. He also saw that the way in which he gained Grant Bovey's trust, and showed a genuine interest in the business, and his understanding of Grant's requirement that Grosvenor should make it easy for him to get additional finance, were crucial elements in the final decision to go with Grosvenor.

A final hectic flurry of phone calls in the half an hour before Grant left for Japan held both suitors at bay until the following week when he got back from Japan.

Grant could see pros and cons to both deals. On the one hand Baronsmead's close relationship with Barclays could be helpful, but on the other, Grosvenor had done more to convince him that they were really interested in his business. As Grant said at the time:

'There isn't a lot to choose between the two and basically it's down to which company we are going to prefer to get into bed with. Grosvenor has tried to win us over by getting close to us and they have done this in a very professional manner. And I must say I have respect for the people who work for Grosvenor. The people at Baronsmead have tried to impress us with their business acumen. They don't care whether we get on with them or not. They have just come in and said we are the best people for you because we understand your business better than the other people and we can offer you a better service.'

But regardless of where his loyalties lay, Grant was utterly cool in his determination to pursue both deals until the point at which he started incurring fees.

Setting up a venture capital is by no means the cheapest way of financing your business. Grant reckoned that once he gave the go ahead to either Baronsmead or Grosvenor there would be legal fees of between £20 000 and £30 000 and a finder's fee of around £25 000 for Rea Brothers, the merchant bank.

The news of Baronsmead's approach to Watershed did not remain a secret. In fact the venture capital bush telegraph wasted no time in reaching Grosvenor who got to know of the Baronsmead offer several days before Grant returned from Japan.

52

Wednesday, 23 October 1991

Lance had tinkered with the deal to take account of the Baronsmead offer. He faxed a revised offer letter* over to Grant, and now wanted a decision from him. Lance is someone who gets his way by negotiation and diplomacy rather than with any outward display of aggression. He rang Grant to put pressure on him to sign and return the offer letter. You have to read between the lines to get the meaning of the message. Lance said, 'The Baronsmead offer is causing us anxiety here.' Meaning: 'We are very cross indeed that there is this other offer on the table'. He then said, 'The pressure on you to do something is very high. It would be nice to have the thing signed.' Meaning: 'If you don't sign this deal pretty damn quick, it might not be there much longer. Sign it or else.' Grant got the message; ten minutes later the letter was signed and faxed back.

Thursday, 24 October 1991.

At Grosvenor's regular Thursday morning progress meeting Robert Drummond was clearly furious that Grosvenor was now in a beauty contest for Watershed with Baronsmead.

No one blamed Grant for pursuing every avenue; what concerned Robert was the similarity between Baronsmead's offer letter and Grosvenor's. Although Robert was quite sure that Barclays had not given any information to Baronsmead, he pointed out with unconcealed irony:

'The people who are making this offer are associated with the bank that won't supply Watershed with the money which it needs to go forward. As you can imagine we were a bit unhappy when we found out that the venture capital associate of this bank was now making an offer which was marginally better than our own.'

Grosvenor had already asked accountants Stoy Hayward to report on Watershed's accounting policies and stock valuation. Now it was time to call in the lawyers and start the long, laborious process of producing a contract which was acceptable to both Grosvenor and Watershed. For this deal Grosvenor was using one of its regular lawyers, Geoffrey Pickerill, at Lawrence Graham.

Monday, 18 November 1991

Geoffrey Pickerill and his assistant Margaret Orgill had prepared a first draft of the agreement. They were now ready to thrash out the details with Grosvenor's Tony Crook and Lance. On the surface, contracts are dry and legalistic, but underneath all that convoluted language a good lawyer will produce an agreement which as well as being legally watertight will also reflect exactly the intended spirit of the deal.

The difficulty with this investment was that it was all about Grant Bovey. The question was how should he be controlled? Geoffrey explained the balance which the legal agreement must strike.

'If you clip his wings then he can't fly, if he flies you can't control him. Grosvenor has to have a great deal of faith that he has the right combination of entrepreneurial flair and business common sense. We will be able to write into the agreement some degree of control, but it is only effective if he cares to observe it. If he decides to disappear in a puff of smoke, there is nothing we can do about it. We will have simply made the wrong investment.'

Lance's main concern was with the tone of the content of certain proposed video projects. He was worried that Grosvenor would have only limited control over the programmes Watershed produces and that the company could start producing videos which Grosvenor would be unhappy to be associated with. Earlier discussions with Watershed revealed that the company intended producing a sex education video, provisionally titled *Lessons in Love* during 1992 to compete with the highly successful *Lovers Guides* which have sold 700 000 copies.

Grosvenor had told Grant it didn't object to the production of a sex education video even though Lance was concerned that this might damage the Watershed brand name. There was no denying that this was a change of direction for Watershed and Lance thought there should be some controls over Grant just in case he was tempted to err over that hard to define line which separates the decent and tasteful from the indecent and exploitative.

As the agreement stood, Grosvenor already had some control over Watershed's output, in that Grant couldn't spend sums of money which put the business at risk without Grosvenor's prior approval. This was designed to prevent Grant signing up a big exclusive rights deal without first informing Grosvenor.

Tony Crook was clearly unhappy about hedging Watershed in with any more conditions and restrictions. As far as he was concerned, less is more; the less you restrict the entrepreneur, the more you are likely to get out of him. This was the main thrust of his thinking as the deal followed its road to completion. On the question of the sex education videos, he was prepared to back Grant's judgement and give him the benefit of the doubt.

It was hardly surprising, given Tony's views on allowing the entrepreneur room to manoeuvre, that Lance's next suggestion was rejected out of hand without any real discussion. Lance had obviously thought a lot as to how to go about writing an agreement in circumstances like these where effectively just one person is being backed. He suggested imposing tight controls on funding which would make it difficult for Watershed to get the money it needed to develop unless it was prepared to pass through various pre-determined hoops. Lance had picked up these ideas in his venture capital training sessions, but, in the end, Tony Crook's more relaxed view prevailed, saying 'We are backing the man.

There should only be sanctions to cover the major problems.'

Even Geoffrey's suggestion that with an annual video output of just 40 titles it ought to be possible for each video to be agreed in advance by the board was pronounced unworkable. Lance pointed out how difficult this would be in practice, given Grant's energetic and sometimes impulsive style of management. He cited as his example Grant's latest idea: videos of Andrew Lloyd Webber shows. The idea had only come to Grant in the previous week. By this week he had already arranged meetings. Grant's way of working often involves making his mind up on the hoof and Lance was concerned that Grant would find such a clause irksome.

The deal was being held up by Watershed's accounts department who were struggling to finish the accounts for the year which ended on 30 June. The audited accounts were promised for 29 November, and Lance hoped to complete the deal during the first week in December.

Friday, 22 November 1991

For the entrepreneur, the legal meeting when both sides of the deal meet with their respective lawyers is among the most stressful. However much you trust the venture capitalist with whom, by now, you have probably developed a good relationship, there is sometimes a fear that the lawyers are about to tie you up in legal knots. Little did Grant know that it was actually Lance who had prepared a potential bombshell. The reality of the situation was that there had been a real shift of power. Grant might not have realized it but, while he was still being courted by Sunset & Vine and Baronsmead, he was calling the shots. Now he had decided to go with Grosvenor, the boot was on the other foot and Lance could turn on the heat.

The meeting took place at the offices of Lawrence Graham in the Strand, a stone's throw from the Law Courts. Compared with Grosvenor's own spartan headquarters in unfashionable Slough, Lawrence Graham's offices are a testimony to the rich pickings of the top corporate solicitors during the boom years of the 1980s.

Grant seemed apprehensive and his tactic was to take the initiative. He wanted things out of this meeting and so he went on the offensive to get them clarified at the beginning. He wanted to set a target date for completing the deal and he wanted new service contracts for himself and Kim Clayton, Watershed's financial director.

Grant couldn't sign the deal with the FA because he couldn't pay for it until the Grosvenor deal was signed and the money was in the bank. He hoped the deal could be completed on 6 December. Grant reassured Tony Crook that the delay in getting both deals signed had not cooled the FA's ardour and that there was no danger of the FA pulling out of the deal.

However, there was still a question mark over the audited accounts and with the 29 November deadline looming they had still not materialized. Nor had Stoy Hayward, the accountants which Grosvenor had put in, produced its report. Both were promised for early the following week and no one saw any objection in aiming for completion on 6 December.

Geoffrey agreed to draw up fresh service contracts for Grant and Kim. To avoid holding up the deal these were to be separately negotiated and wouldn't form part of the formal agreement between Watershed and Grosvenor.

Lance didn't believe for one minute that Grant was going to start putting his feet up as soon as the Grosvenor money hit his bank account, but on the other hand he wanted to be absolutely sure which was why he was now introducing this performance incentive into the deal. Grosvenor was now asking for the right to take 50 per cent of Watershed's profits if the venture capitalist couldn't realize its investment and made an exit in three and half years' time. This was a draconian measure designed to keep Grant on his toes. He was now under no misapprehension as to what was expected of him, because the consequences of failing to achieve exit within this time scale were nothing short of punitive.

Grant had no idea that Lance was planning to spring this on him. However, he was confident enough about Watershed's ability to continue to grow that he decided to let it go through almost on the nod. As he said Grosvenor's involvement in Watershed was not going to dampen his appetite to succeed and he was looking to make his own exit within the time frame proposed by Grosvenor so there was no point him going to the stake for the principle.

Grant was saving his fire for a later clause which placed restrictions on his right to sell his shares in Watershed. No venture capitalist in this situation is going to give an entrepreneur the unfettered right to sell their shares. As Geoffrey reiterated: 'We are investing in you and if you sell your shares then the company ceases to be of interest to us.' He suggested loosening the straightjacket to give Grant the right to sell up to 10 per cent of his holding without asking Grosvenor's permission.

Lance knew from his venture capital training that it is a basic tenet of his trade that you don't give the entrepreneur you are backing such a comfortable lifestyle that he no longer has any incentive to push the business forward. Lance said with this kind of agreement, Grant could sell, say one per cent of his shares each year, and give himself a reason to stay at home with his feet up.

Now Grant was forced to come clean. At some stage he wanted to move house and he was counting on being able to sell some of his shares in order to help finance the move. It was not his intention to sell shares in order to boost his income. Tony Crook said it was not a problem and it was agreed to find a form of words which could cover this eventuality. This venture capitalist was determined he should stay really hungry.

Another problem for Grant was sorting out Watershed's day-to-day banking requirements. Grosvenor had asked Grant to get his bank to confirm in writing that the bank overdraft would be increased to £250 000 once the funding from Grosvenor was in place. The bank were prepared to give a verbal undertaking but it wouldn't put anything in writing. This is the kind of chicken and egg situation which can cause endless delays with the venture capitalist refusing to move until it has a written undertaking from the bank and the bank refusing to move until it sees the venture capitalist's money. In this case Grant asked Tony Crook to intervene to break the stalemate and after talking to the bank, Grosvenor decided to push on with the deal on the basis of a verbal agreement from the bank.

Lance was going on holiday. His offer to delay his holiday and see the deal through was turned down by Tony Crook. As he left to catch his plane he asked for a word with Tony, and Geoffrey – in effect a huddled conversation in the corridor. Whispered conversations like these could almost have been designed to set the entrepreneur's nerves on edge. Grant chewed his pencil anxiously. In fact nothing of much consequence was discussed except Tony's desire to resolve the issue of the Castle shares. The thought that Castle might still be shareholders after Grosvenor became involved worried him.

Lance had already agreed to have a word with Grant before he left but was aware of the effect that Tony, Geoffrey and his secret, but ever so visible, meeting was having on Grant. As he went he walked down the corridor with Grant, offering him almost fatherly reassurance that all the hard work they had done behind the scenes was bearing fruit and that the deal was going fine and he had nothing to worry about.

The meeting wound down. Grant felt more confident and brought everyone up to date on recent developments. The Scottish Football Association had approached him about doing an exclusive deal. Grant was thinking of offering £135 000 a year, guaranteed for three years. However news of the deal had filtered out and other video production companies were interested. Grant hoped to shut out the competition by getting the Scottish Football Association to agree to a deal, subject to contract, which would give him the breathing space to make sure all the sums really did add up.

On the face of it the deal looked promising. To begin with the Scottish Football Association had always retained the rights to any filming, so Watershed wouldn't have to negotiate to buy the footage from the BBC. No videos of the Scottish FA cup final or the Scotland team had ever been released, so there was plenty of material to exploit. In addition to which the Scottish buy more videos per head than anyone else. But the Scottish FA might decide to give the cup final winner the right to exploit the video rights to the cup final match. If that happened the deal was a lot less valuable to Watershed and the offer would be scaled down accordingly.

Geoffrey was pleased with the way the meeting had gone:

'It was an easier ride than I expected. We quite often get

problems with the lawyers for the other side especially when they don't do this type of work. But in this case there were no histrionics, and no particular disagreements. It means we can continue to build the partnership.'

However, Friday, 6 December, came and went, and still the deal was not signed.

Tuesday, 10 December 1991.

Once again everyone assembled at the offices of Lawrence Graham. Grant had another meeting and arrived late, looking tired; the whole process of getting this deal signed had gone on too long, and with his cash flow now stretched to bursting the creditors were getting restless. What Grant didn't realize was that he had had a relatively easy ride. Grant might be exhausted but he was one of the lucky ones. Getting a venture capital deal signed, sealed and delivered in just over two months is a lot better than most companies can expect. Even so there was a vague feeling of unease about him. Was the deal ever going to get done? Was life with Grosvenor going to be an endless round of senseless meetings? If so, then much of the fun of running Watershed was going to disappear.

There were still questions to be sorted out. Watershed agreed the FA deal way back in January but the agreement still hadn't been signed. Grant explained the signing had been delayed by the absence of the FA's Glen Kirton, in the United States.

On the Grosvenor side, the Stoy Hayward report still hadn't arrived. It was due the following day and no one envisaged that this was going to throw up any particular problems. As Geoffrey pointed out the accountants would have warned Grosvenor if there was anything in Watershed's accounting policies which had given them cause for concern.

The deal was still not ready to be signed, but diaries were checked, and 5.00 p.m. on Thursday, 12 December was looking a distinct possibility.

The only thing which might still sabotage the deal was Grant's objection to the way Grosvenor intended calculating his bonus. He discovered that his bonus was to be linked to growth in profits rather than actual profits. Grant believes in incentives. He was even prepared to accept a lower salary and a higher bonus so long as the bonus was linked to profits not profits' growth. He was looking several years down the line, when profits might well have grown to around £2 million a year. The company could then find they had reached a plateau and there could be a couple of years when profits hardly grew at all. In these circumstances the company would be earning very high profits but Grant would find himself without a bonus.

Grosvenor dug their heels in. Grant was adamant that he didn't like it but it was decided to pull back from this particular precipice and discuss it again once the deal was signed. When the issue was finally resolved a compromise was reached with half Grant's bonus related to profits, the other half to profits' growth.

Thursday, 12 December 1991

Six days later than originally planned, everyone was once again assembled at the offices of Lawrence Graham. Much to everyone's obvious relief the deal was finally being signed, the pile of documents was nearly a foot deep. Geoffrey ticked them off his checklist – there were at least twenty documents: a subscription agreement, deed of covenant, articles of association, a disclosure letter, the Castle contract, the RCA contract, the Virgin contract, the list seemed endless. Suddenly, it was all over; the deal was done and the champagne corks popped.

The look of pleasure on Lance's face said it all. This was his first deal and he had pulled it off without too many hitches. However, his relief in getting the deal signed was tempered with sadness that his involvement with Watershed was now coming to an end. His greatest fear was that Grant would run very much faster than anybody else in the company and that he would leave the company behind. But as he said:

'It's Tony Crook's job to make sure this doesn't happen and that the organization grows with him. I'm very fond of the company, and I would love to spend a day a week down there

making sure that things are going in the right direction but it just isn't possible. Tony will spend closer to half a day a month there. Barely enough time to make up his mind.'

And what were Grant's feelings now that the months of negotiations were over?

'A mixture of emotions. Relief that it is now all over, because you reach a point when you think this is not ever going to end. Elation that we have managed to get through another stage of the company's development. It's also a weight off my mind. But this isn't the end of something, this is the beginning. The hard work for the lawyers, the advisers has ended. The hard work for Watershed Pictures is just beginning.'

And had he changed his mind about venture capital over the last four months?

'What you don't realize is that it is always touch and go. It soon becomes evident that the venture capitalist can pull the plug at any point during the negotiations. Instead of my confidence growing after the offer letter was sent it actually diminished. It should be the reverse, but when you get into the real negotiations and the process of accountants' reports and all the other rigmarole they have to go through, your confidence in them actually doing the deal starts to diminish because you realize just how many things can go wrong. Venture capitalists are very volatile. I always felt I might say something which they didn't like; they could think about it for ten minutes and then turn round and say they had changed their minds. In the meetings you are being asked all sorts of questions, but you are having to think politics before you answer them. So in the final stages of the negotiation, the person who is trying to raise the money is under a lot of pressure.

'I still think that venture capital is an essential part of the business community. But don't even think of talking to a venture capital company with a faint heart. If you do they will walk all over you. You have to have conviction in your company's ability to do what you say it is going to do and conviction in your own abilities to stand up and argue with them because that is what they will do. It's hard, it's tough and it gets aggressive and you have to be equally as aggressive in the way you negotiate for the rights of your company. If they spot a hint of weakness in your character they will home in on it and make the most of it.

'There were days when if you had asked me what I thought of venture capital, I would have said this is awful, I wouldn't have advised anyone to get into this. But now it's all over, I can say I enjoyed it. We will put it behind us now and put it down to experience.

Grant Bovey's advice to other entrepreneurs seeking venture capital is don't take anything for granted, don't underestimate the cost.

'When you get your offer letter don't make the mistake of thinking that the offer is in the bag. The offer letter is only the opening shot. This is when the serious negotiations really start, so don't expect the final offer to look anything like the first offer. It is not uncommon for venture capitalists to change the deal at the completion meeting. Don't count on the money until it finally hits your bank account.

'Getting venture capital is extremely time consuming and deals are rarely concluded as quickly as you hope. Most small businesses are extremely dependent on the work of one or two key individuals and if these people are putting a lot of energy into raising capital they can end up neglecting their business. Entrepreneurs going for venture capital should be aware that this is a very real danger, and I am convinced that Watershed could have earned more if I hadn't been so tied up raising money for those two months.

'The costs can be enormous too. In my case I was raising £500 000 but £81 000 of that went straight out in fees, a much higher figure than the £65 000 which I originally estimated. There was £20 000 to Rea Brothers, £8000 for my auditors,

£3000 for a financial adviser, £17 000 to Stoy Hayward who did the accountants' investigation, £16 000 for Grosvenor's legal fees, £12 000 for our own solicitor and finally a £5000 completion fee to Grosvenor, bringing the total to £81 000, around 16 per cent of the money we raised.'

Watershed is a company which has grown rapidly over a very short period. The figures show the progress of sales and profits since the company was formed towards the end of 1988.

	Six months to 30.6.89	Year to 30.6.90	Year to 30.6.91	Year to 30.6.92
Sales	£265 000	£737 000	£2.2m	£3.6m
Profits (loss)	(£90 000)	£96 000	£200 000	£450 000

The year to the end of June 1992 was disappointing. Grant had hoped to make profits of £800 000, but these failed to materialize and by Christmas 1992 Watershed had hit further problems and Grosvenor provided more funds and insisted on the right to appoint a chairman.

Grant is now swinging the emphasis of his business away from video and into television production. He has high hopes of an exclusive UK television rights deal which he has signed with Nigel Mansell and the Newman Haas team that will bring IndyCar racing to British television screens in 1993.

Chapter Five

Early's of Witney

Early's is thought to be the second oldest company in the country. It has been making blankets on the same site in Witney in Oxfordshire since 1669. Early's is a brand name which is synonymous with all that is best in British blankets and for much of the last 300 years it has been a traditional family-run business.

Witney, the home of Britain's blanket industry, is a small industrial town set in the heart of the Oxfordshire countryside. Over the last 20 years, however, the blanket business in the United Kingdom has been gradually undermined by the popularity of the continental quilt, and Early's is now the last remaining blanket maker in Witney.

In the late 1980s the company brought in John Wilson to restructure its manufacturing base. A Lancastrian, John Wilson was recruited for his knowledge of manufacturing, particularly of cotton and polyester bedlinen. The company was keen to exploit the Early's brand name with a range of bed linen for the home market and this was John Wilson's area of expertise. There were also plans to expand export sales for blankets in those areas of the world where blankets are still popular.

In May 1990 Early's was acquired by Grovewood Securities, an industrial holding company which was being turned into a property company by entrepreneur David Holland. Grovewood had no interest in blankets, but liked the look of Early's 60-acre land bank in and around Witney. This had been accumulated following the merger of Witney's two biggest blanket makers way back in the 1960s. A decision to concentrate all Early's manufacturing and distribution on one site had left the company with a huge amount of land which it no longer needed.

Grovewood never made any secret of the fact that it was only interested in the property, so in December 1990 when John Wilson and his management team proposed a management buy-out of the blanket business, Grovewood encouraged them to go out and look for the finance.

Raising finance for a management buy-out is a slow and laborious process. There is the preparation of a plausible business plan and then there is the endless round of meetings with financiers until you have one hooked. Grosvenor was approached by John Wilson's advisers, the accountants, Grant Thornton in June 1991. It was a relatively simple deal: Grovewood were keen to sell and the price was right.

It was the kind of simple, uncomplicated deal which venture capitalists love – the dream deal which can be completed in six weeks from the day the proposal first walks through the venture capitalists' door. In July, Grovewood agreed in principle to sell the business to the managers for £3 million with Grosvenor providing the venture capital.

In July the deal to sell to the managers fell by the wayside when Grovewood decided to look for a buyer who would pay a higher price. In December 1990 when John Wilson first approached Grovewood there was no sense of urgency, no sense that here was a deal which had to be completed tomorrow. By August the climate had changed dramatically. What had looked like superficial cracks in the property company Priest Marrians was a deal too far.

The possibility of exploiting Early's surplus land receded and the managers of the manufacturing side became increasingly concerned by rumours that Grovewood were in financial trouble. Alarm bells rang when the parent company started plundering the manufacturing company's healthy cash flow. And life became even tougher when the company's bankers, in an attempt to stop this, froze the accounts of all the subsidiary companies.

John Wilson was now desperate to separate Early's blanket business from its ailing parent. If Grovewood was heading for receivership, John Wilson did not want Early's to go down with it.

Healthy companies like Early's can survive receivership, but it is never good for business and John Wilson feared that if Early's went into receivership alongside Grovewood, blanket orders would dry up.

For all its apparent simplicity, Early's was very nearly the deal which got away. Three times the deal got to within a whisker of being signed. Each time it was aborted at the very last moment. The deal was finally signed on 3 December 1991, six long months after the initial approach. It is hard to imagine the gamut of emotions which the management team and Grosvenor experienced during these months.

Early's demonstrates just how fragile these deals are. Vendors who can't get the agreement of bankers to sell, documentation which goes wrong, aggressive venture capitalists; these are the factors which held up the Early's deal. But it could have been almost anything. It left John Wilson and his team feeling like helpless outsiders, powerless and bemused as they watched their business and livelihood reduced to a pile of paper shuffled from one out tray to another.

Grant Bovey at Watershed described how vulnerable he felt and that the overriding atmosphere which pervaded all those endless meetings was one of sheer volatility, as if the whole thing could simply blow up in his face with no warning. It should be a reminder to anyone who is thinking of going for venture capital that no deal is worth the paper it is printed on until it is finally signed, sealed and delivered and the money is safely in the account.

Grosvenor's executive, Trevor Bayley, takes up the story from the beginning:

'When Early's first approached us, they were talking to Barclays with a view to getting a mortgage-backed facility. The price of the deal was £3.6 million of which £2.5 million was to come from mortgaging the property which was worth £3.5 million. They were having difficulty raising the money from their regular bankers, so they approached Royal Bank of Scotland who agreed to provide a mortgage of £1.6 million.

'Grovewood originally imposed an end of July deadline for completion. But in the middle of July, Grovewood suddenly withdrew from the deal and extended the deadline until the end of August.

'It transpired that it was touting the business around looking for another company to buy the business and top the offer the management buy-out team were making. Grovewood were obviously under a great deal of pressure themselves. Their share price was going down, they had large debts and there were all sorts of rumours doing the rounds as to what was going to happen to the company.

'Grovewood did receive an offer in excess of the management team's offer, but the buyer made it very clear he was not prepared to go ahead with a disenfranchised management and obviously, given the fact that there was an MBO on the table, he was only prepared to take the business if he had the full support of the management team.

67

'Towards the end of August it looked as if we were getting there. I became convinced that we could do the deal on 6 September. We had reached agreement with Grovewood on just about every issue. Negotiations between ourselves and the management team were progressing well. But then we ran up against access problems to the factory site and we started to have problems getting any sort of response from Grovewood. The press was rife with rumours about what was happening to Grovewood.

'It soon became clear that it wasn't Grovewood's management who were responsible for conducting negotiations, it was the two institutions which held the charge on the property, Nykredit, a Scandinavian financial institution, and the Midland Bank, and the deal which had been agreed between the management and Grovewood was not sufficiently sweet to satisfy the bankers so the whole deal was shelved.

'Two or three weeks later the board of Early's of Witney PLC put the company into receivership and a week later the parent company followed suit.

'Since then, the receiver, Price Waterhouse, has been marketing the Early's business, generating a lot of interest from various people well known in the industry. The deal has now changed considerably. Originally we were going to take Early's holding company and subsidiaries and all the assets and liabilities. Now we are just taking certain specific assets. We put in an offer £2.1 million but it wasn't accepted. We increased it to £2.3 million with an added sweetner that if the company could take a pensions holiday the receiver would receive some of the proceeds, and the receiver accepted it.'

68

Monday, 18 November 1991

The original deal with the management team was structured five months ago in June and July when the deal was worth £3 million. It gave Grosvenor a 60 per cent stake with a ratchet mechanism which worked in both directions giving Early's management a smaller or larger stake than their initial 40 per cent depending on performance.

Grosvenor now wanted to alter the structure. The overall cost was to be lowered, but then Grosvenor was actually putting in more. It wanted a greater initial slug of the business to allow for this and the fact that the company had been in receivership for two months.

John Wilson, his adviser Andrew Tacon from Grant Thornton, and Karl Lang, the financial director from Earlys, went to Grosvenor to finalize the deal. Trevor had set himself a Friday deadline for completion. He expected Grant Thornton would warn John Wilson that it was likely Grosvenor would want to renegotiate their stake.

Trevor proposed that the management should reduce their initial stake from 40 per cent to one-third, with Grosvenor having an initial two-thirds stake in the business. To soften the blow, he suggested altering the terms of the ratchet to remove the possibility that the management could have their stake further diluted. Under the old agreement, if Early's had failed to perform, the management's stake in the business would have been reduced to just

20 per cent. Under the new proposal it could never go below one-third.

Trevor hoped the management team would see that the restructuring meant that while the deal was now better for Grosvenor it was no worse for them. However, he realized he might have a fight on his hands, so instead of tackling the issue head on he let John Wilson and Andrew Tacon take the initiative.

They discussed the Early's pension fund, which was not as healthy as originally thought and which might threaten the company's ability to take a pension holiday and the receiver's sweetner. Maxwell's plundering of the Mirror group pension funds may be the worst example of a troubled business using its pension fund as a source of finance, but it is by no means unique. Many ailing companies have used their pension schemes perfectly legally. Grovewood was no exception. Early's pension scheme had had to write off £650 000 invested in Grovewood. It also paid £300 000 for six tied cottages owned by Early's which were unlet and producing no income.

Grosvenor wanted a non-executive chairman who could dedicate a couple of days a week to Early's, at least during the first six months when the company started implementing its business plan which involved a big push for overseas sales. Trevor told John Wilson that Grosvenor wanted to appoint John Booker the company doctor*, who had been chosen for his experience of restructuring companies coming out of receivership. He had already been sent the business plan and the next step was for him to meet the management team to see if they could work together.

Trevor then dropped his bombshell and it was soon very clear that John Wilson had no idea that a fundamental restructuring of the deal was on the cards for this meeting. He thought he was there to finalize the details and to check over the fine print. He was not well pleased to find that there was a hidden agenda. Totally unprepared, he felt he should have been warned in advance. But pressure to complete the deal was mounting and Grosvenor effectively had him over a barrel. So he had no other option but to agree. The previous week Grosvenor had given him the impression that the extra money was going in as loan stock; there had been no suggestion that they wanted to alter the management's share in the business.

Hurt and puzzled, John Wilson looked for some support from Andrew Tacon. However, Andrew took a more sanguine view and it was agreed that John Wilson should discuss the revised deal with the entire MBO team and that he would telephone Grosvenor later in the day.

A weary John Wilson left the meeting to return to Witney commenting that, after nearly eight months, it would be a nice feeling to get back to doing business rather than raising finance.

Grosvenor thought it was a business which had potential and solid asset-backing. Under John Wilson the workforce had been slimmed down from 500 to 140 with the manufacturing now all concentrated on one site. The business has high fixed costs which makes it very sensitive to movements in volume. Over the last twenty years the company had suffered severe competition from the continental quilt. However, if it was successful in its aim of attracting much higher overseas sales and diversifying its product range, it should have no difficulty in boosting sales. Early's sells eight out of ten of all blankets sold to the public in UK shops. It already sells in around 40 countries, but in only a handful does it win more than £100 000 of orders a year.

Friday, 29 November 1991

Trevor's timetable had now slipped a week, but hopes were running high that the deal would be completed today, and Early's could once again start trading as a manufacturing company free from the interference of troublesome parents. The new terms had been agreed by the management team, although at the cost of one of the original members who decided not to participate. The management team was putting in £200 000 and the other members were going to make up the shortfall caused by the withdrawal of one of their team.

But that was last week's problem. Today, as everyone assembled at the offices of solicitors, Lawrence Graham, it emerged that there was a major hiccup and that completion could be heading for the sands. It seemed that the Midland Bank and Nykredit, had failed to reach agreement as to how the proceeds of the sale should be divided.

The fear arose that Grosvenor might reduce the price of the deal if there was any further delay. Grosvenor wondered why the banks were imposing a condition which they knew Grosvenor couldn't accept and which gave the impression that it was Grosvenor who was now causing the delay.

Nykredit refused to release its charge on the property in a way which was acceptable to Grosvenor, but was prepared to give an undertaking that the charge would be released the following day. Grosvenor were only prepared to accept such an undertaking if it was signed by Nykredit's lawyers, one of the City's top firms of solicitors, but they had failed to turn up at the meeting and refused to sign any such undertaking.

Michael Glover was there to sign the deal for Grosvenor and was absolutely furious. He was determined that no one should think that Grosvenor was acting unreasonably. He might have been prepared to accept the risk that Nykredit would take the money and then not release the charge if he had been dealing with a UK clearing bank. But everyone agreed that Grosvenor would be mad to put its faith in a Scandinavian bank which was known to be pulling out of the UK.

The solicitors for Nykredit claimed that their power of attorney which gave them the authority to sign an undertaking on behalf of Nykredit had run out, but there was a strong suspicion that they were as unwilling as Grosvenor to put themselves at risk. And the director of Nykredit who could release the charge had returned to Denmark.

Lawrence Graham partner, Caroline Janzen, Grosvenor's solicitor, confirmed Michael's suspicions that fewer and fewer deals, even those involving the clearing banks, were completed with such undertakings. In a recession purchasers simply don't want to put their money at risk, even for a day, and it is now much more common for any charges on assets to be released on completion.

Michael Glover often finds himself cast as the hard man of Grosvenor and there are times when the situation demands someone who can act both decisively and dangerously. At 8.30 p.m., with just two and a half hours before his own power of attorney to sign the deal for Grosvenor expired and no longer convinced that the banks wanted to do the deal, he and Trevor went off to the pub leaving the lawyers to sort out the mess.

John Wilson and the management team were due to arrive an hour before. They finally turned up after a nightmare journey which had started on Oxford station with their train being cancelled and ended, after an hour spent in a London traffic jam, with their arrival at the offices of Lawrence Graham in the Strand. The superstitious would have called it divine intervention; perhaps they should have taken it as a sign. They thought they were on the point of taking charge of their own destiny; they found themselves giving orders for pizza.

Suddenly there was a chink of light. The lawyers agreed to accept certain faxed documents; miraculously, Nykredit's solicitors' power of attorney had been extended. It was now down to Nykredit. Would it be prepared to accept an undertaking from the new management's lawyers that the funds would be in its account first thing on Monday when the charge on the property was released?

A search party was sent to look for Michael and Trevor. A trawl of ten local pubs failed to locate them. Their absence was tactical but as the evening grew longer, the lawyers showed signs of irritation. Then just as suddenly the pair returned. But the deal was no closer to completion. Nykredit was only prepared to sign if the new management's lawyers could produce a banker's draft or cash. Although how they were meant to get a banker's draft for £2.3 million at 11.00 p.m. on a Friday night wasn't clear. Did Nykredit really think that lawyers travelled with banker's drafts in their back pockets and suitcases full of ready money? As Michael pointed out, what they were really saying was that they didn't trust the lawyers.

The arrival of the pizzas provided a few moments of light relief with some joker asking who had the power of attorney to release the pizzas.

Michael had become very angry and nothing seemed to appease him. Even Caroline's suggestion that the deal was signed and that the funds are held in escrow by the lawyers until Monday was rejected. Michael wanted the deal completed there and then on his terms. As he said: 'It is just assumed we will provide the finance when convenient. But it may not be convenient to do the deal on Monday.'

Suddenly the room was packed. Michael pinned everyone to the wall with the sheer force of his anger. Telling them he had never come across such a fiasco:

'We have had the funds available since August. Last week we agreed we would push for a completion today. We agreed two and a half weeks ago that getting the charges released was going to be tricky, and still it hasn't been sorted out. It is still a good deal but costs are escalating, surely the banks must know that the price is going down. I won't put money into a company just to have it sucked out of the top right hand drawer in expenses.'

73

Having vented his fury and frustration, Michael had to accept that the deal wouldn't be done that night. It was agreed to do it during normal banking hours on Tuesday when all the paper work was finally sorted out and the banks had agreed their deed of priority.

It was a frustrating evening for John Wilson and his management team. They expected to leave as the proud owners of their business. Instead, they found themselves hovering functionless on the periphery, as lawyers argued with lawyers and banks and venture capitalists dug their heels in. It all seemed so remote from the real world. A world in which a factory, a full quarter of a mile long, produces a million and a quarter blankets a year.

Congealed slabs of half-eaten pizza in their greasy boxes summed up the day's dereliction.

Tuesday, 3 December 1991

'Everyone agrees that the deal needs to be done today. On Tuesday, everyone wants to do the deal,' is how Michael Glover explained the differences in mood between Friday and today. And there was no doubt that as everyone gathered once again in the offices of solicitors Lawrence Graham, the atmosphere was positive and optimistic. The rancour of Friday had disappeared as the long drawn out ritual of the signing got under way. Lawrence Graham partner, Geoffrey Pickerill, urged them to get cracking, 'There are two trolleys outside, one coffee and one champagne, which one I bring in depends on how fast you get on with it.'

There wasn't enough room at the table. The ever self-effacing John Wilson signed his documents on his lap huddled in a chair in the corner of the room. When the documents had been signed Trevor left for an urgent appointment at his son's first birthday party. Sometime later, Early's sent his son a specially-embroidered Witney blanket to commemorate the date.

74

Traumatic is how John Wilson described the process of getting venture capital. And what advice would he give those who are contemplating a management buy-out? 'Make absolutely sure you have a vendor who wishes to sell and more importantly is able to sell. This is really where we ran into serious problems.'

Since Grosvenor invested, Early's has continued to restructure it's business. It seems the business was damaged by its period in receivership more than anyone had realized. The company has not been trading as successfully as expected and won't meet its profit forecast for 1992 but development and investment in the company has continued. In October 1992 the sales team was strengthened with the recruitment of a new sales director, John Foster from Osman, part of the Dorma Household Textile group. At the same time, chairman John Booker – his job now completed – was replaced by Peter Haworth, the former chief executive of the Sekers Furnishing Textile group.

Chapter Six

Direct Vision Rental

Direct Vision Rental (DVR) is a video and television rental company which is pioneering a sales method that undercuts the big high street names, Radio Rentals and Granada, by as much as £5 a month.

DVR is the brainchild of Brian Hopper who has already made one fortune selling a small chain of video rental shops to Rediffusion.

DVR cuts prices to the bone because it sells directly to the public which eliminates the need to maintain a costly presence in the high street. Advertising is done via leaflets which are inserted into free newspapers and delivered to people's homes. Potential customers are given a freephone number to ring, and if an order is placed, a credit check is run, and the video or television is then delivered either the following day or at a time arranged with the customer.

When Grosvenor became involved, DVR still owned two shops; Video Viewpoint in Dunstable and Mastervision in Enfield. Brian Hopper also runs another business, Look-In TV, with one shop in Aylesbury which he owns jointly with his long standing business partner Graham Littler.

But it is DVR's direct rental business which is expanding fast and which Brian Hopper wanted Grosvenor to back. He came to Grosvenor because he needed to expand his capital base – the amount of money he had invested in the business – before the banks would lend him the enormous sums which would be needed to expand his operation into new areas. He wanted to set up new depots to serve the North West and the East Midlands.

Getting a venture capitalist to back his business was the bait he needed to hook the bank. But the amount of money he now needed was of a different magnitude and the decision to lend had to be taken at the highest level within the bank. Without the bank's support Brian could forget his plans for a fast expansion which explained why it was so important to get the venture capitalists on board, not so much for the amount of money they would bring but more because the bank's coffers would only open if the venture capitalists were persuaded this was a business worth backing.

The rate of expansion had surprised even Brian Hopper who explained how it all came about:

'We had a shop and we dropped leaflets around the surrounding area. We found we attracted customers from about 20 miles away and what we very soon learnt was that a lot respond over the telephone. They didn't need to come into the shop. Most of the orders were taken over the telephone.

'Then we found that once we had installed the equipment in a customer's house if it went wrong they didn't bother to come back to the shop, they picked up the telephone for a service call instead. As they were paying by banker's order they had no need to come in to make payments. So I suddenly twigged that, really, why do we need a shop at all. And that's how the whole DVR operation started.

'I have been in television rental for a number of years with a shop in Dunstable and another in Enfield. We started the direct rental in October 1989 from above one of our shops in a room which was literally ten by ten. From the moment we started we were absolutely staggered at how well it went. Within three weeks we were renting out hundreds of videos and televisions a week.

'The premises were bursting at the seams with girls sitting on the stairs filling in proposal forms. The morale of the staff and the way everyone mixed in was absolutely fantastic. After three weeks I realized I had to get some extra office accommodation. By the November I was certain we had this

wonderful success on our hands. But I also realized the idea was so simple that someone could copy it. So we went out and identified new depots to cover the Kent and Hampshire areas and by January we had them up and running.'

Brian had an infectious enthusiasm for what he was doing which clearly inspired everyone who worked with him. His is a classic rags to riches story. He had been in the television rental business for over twenty years but he started his working life as a television engineer and he was the first member of his family to go into business. However, in the world of high finance people like Brian Hopper, who never learn to disguise their humble origins or care to acquire a veneer of sophistication, are often surprised when negotiations fall into some black hole of class superiority.

This is the story of the deal which nearly disappeared into the ether, not for want of a good business idea – Brian Hopper has that – but simply because he speaks a different language from the financiers, bankers and accountants whom he had to deal with in his attempts to raise money and this made them feel uneasy.

He made certain fundamental mistakes which nearly cost him the deal. Brian and his managers at DVR were not equipped to prepare the kind of documents which are needed to hook a venture capitalist. He hired two young advisers, Craig Bonner and William Flynn who, while they are known on the fringes of the venture capital world, were viewed by Grosvenor in a poor light.

This was the first time that Brian had ever embarked on such an ambitious fund-raising exercise and the first time he had needed to employ advisers. With little or no experience of what to expect, it was Brian's bad luck to choose advisers who failed to win the confidence of the venture capitalists. As Robert Drummond said early on in the negotiations: 'The intermediaries are not helping him, they are actually damaging his case, because they are selling it too strongly.'

Brian was not aware until the deal was all but complete that Grosvenor had reservations about his advisers. But it was not just a question of the hard sell. At one crucial point Brian didn't appear to understand the deal which may have been due to a lack of communication between him and his advisers.

Brian saw it differently:

'I couldn't have done it without Craig Bonner and William Flynn. We needed them to prepare the business plans and cash flow forecasts and to present the information in the way venture capitalists expect. There was no way we could have done this for ourselves.'

With or without his advisers, Brian somehow always failed to hit quite the right note. When he was left to his own devices he rode roughshod over the accounting sensibilities of the accountant from the big city firm which was sent to investigate DVR which not surprisingly resulted in a damning report that threatened to abort the deal at the eleventh hour.

Grosvenor was first introduced to DVR by two other venture capitalists, Candover and ECI, who were both considering investing. Half the company belongs to Brian Hopper; his long-time colleague Graham Littler has 45 per cent and operations director John Nelson has five per cent. Graham Littler had worked with Brian for 20 years, and they had been friends for even longer, having met while doing National Service. They have a deep admiration for each other, but Graham had decided that he would now like to let up a bit and had decided not to take an active part in the new direct selling operation.

So DVR was now run by Brian Hopper, who is the chief executive; Eddie Crisp, the quiet finance director who seemed happier with a column of figures than in the management meetings, and John Nelson, a small dynamo of a man whose job it was to get the new warehouses up and running.

Monday, 2 December 1991

Janis Anderson from Grosvenor visited DVR's offices above a fitted bedroom shop in Dunstable knowing that Robert Drummond liked what he had seen of the company on paper. She was reassured by DVR's spartan offices which indicated that here was a company which believed in keeping a tight lid on costs. Brian

Hopper introduced her to the saleswomen and took her through the stages between an order being taken and the instruction arriving at the warehouse.

Brian also took the opportunity to ram home the message that his ten telephone saleswomen were pulling in sales which traditional rental operations would need 100 high street shops to achieve. Credit checking was simple, quick and according to Brian extremely effective. As Brian said he only wanted blue chip customers, so they had to be in full time employment, on the electoral register, have household insurance, be prepared to pay by standing order and have no record of county court judgements. These policies are applied without exception and had kept the arrears level down. At the time Grosvenor became involved they were running at two per cent. By the autumn of 1992 they had fallen even further with around 0.7 per cent of customers two months behind with their payments and 1.7 per cent having missed one payment. Eddie Crisp, DVR's finance director, explained the computer system and how arrears were not allowed to build up – a polite letter was sent after one month's missed payment, a termination letter after two months and the equipment was then collected at some time over the next month.

John Nelson had been responsible for the siting of new depots and getting them up and running. He explained the DVR philosophy:

'We judge an area not by how large it is, but by how many people we can reach, so we use time maps rather than distance maps when we are looking for places to site a new depot. This leads us to look for sites near motorways and away from city centres, where our drivers get snarled up in traffic.'

Janis's mission was fact-finding. She met Brian's advisers, Craig Bonner, a near chain-smoking young Scot and his associate, William Flynn. They saw it rather differently. Brian was impatient. He had just spent seven weeks negotiating with Candover, the management buy-out specialists, and while Candover were still interested in investing in the company they had decided that they had too much other work and that they did not want to lead the deal. Brian was extremely anxious to push Grosvenor forward quickly so he could get his new depots up and running soon after Christmas.

Janis's painstaking efforts to extract the information she needed, such as which bankers were backing DVR and for how much, what the arrangements were for separating the direct marketing business from the two shops and whether a non-executive chairman was acceptable, were all answered perfectly adequately.

It was just that Brian, either out of sheer enthusiasm for his business, or because his advisers had told him that he needed always to accentuate the positive, never missed an opportunity to present his business in a glowing light. For example he could run his new depots with no extra management; his business was arresting the decline in the rental market because renting was now cheaper than buying. He was full of little dicta – the kind American businessmen have framed on their desks – such as 'You must never ever cheat the customer. Give the customer value for money and he will stay with you for ever.'

Video rental dies a death in the summer, so Brian wanted his new depots up and running for the best part of what he calls the dark months of January, February and March. Most video rental businesses expect to do three-quarters of their business in the six months from October through to March. Brian was pushing Grosvenor to sign the deal on 20 December which gave Janis less than three weeks to complete her investigations and have the accountants run through the books and the lawyer draw up the agreements.

In order to get the accountants and lawyers working on the deal before an offer letter went out, the meeting finished with Craig Bonner agreeing to indemnify Grosvenor for the cost of the accountants and lawyers if the deal didn't go through.

Janis went back to London relatively optimistic:

'It does seem an extremely straightforward business. I need to do a bit more digging around and find out a bit more about the market to get comfortable with it, but it makes

sense that people will move towards rental if it is so much cheaper than outright purchase. You do have the potential problem of other people getting into the market, but if they can grow fast enough, then you can become national before anybody else does.'

However, she did have reservations. She liked and admired Brian Hopper's enthusiasm but at that stage she wondered whether he and his team had the management experience to take DVR into the big league and she was worried about the accounting policies. She didn't know what advice Brian Hopper had been given on how to handle venture capitalists, but whatever it was, he apparently failed to appreciate that Grosvenor would need to dig deeply into the business before it came to a decision and that any attempt to gloss over potential problem areas would be found out in the end.

Wednesday, 4 December 1991

Janis had a meeting with her colleagues, Robert Drummond and Michael Glover, to discuss DVR. Over the course of the last two days, Janis's ardour for the company had cooled. ECI, one of the other venture capitalists involved, had asked an industry expert who had worked for Granada, to take a look at DVR. ECI had told Janis that he had questioned DVR's accounting policies and Brian Hopper's management ability.

In a rental company, getting the accounting policies right is as important as having a good marketing idea. For example rental companies can manipulate their profit figures by playing around with the amount of money they put aside each year for depreciation. If a company is cautious, it puts a lot of money aside for depreciation and declares a low profit figure.

But the same company can show much higher profits if it puts less money aside for depreciation. ECI was not worried by DVR's depreciation policy. DVR used to write its videos and televisions off over eight years. It had now switched to writing them off over the shorter period of six years which was standard for the industry. ECI was rather more concerned at DVR's practice of spreading the costs of installation over a number of years rather than charging them as they occurred which was what the rest of the industry did.

There was also a question mark over how the volume discounts which DVR obtained on its supplies of videos and televisions were treated in the accounts. DVR took the discount as income and put the equipment on to the balance sheet at full cost, not the price actually paid. This gave DVR's profits a boost in the early years when it was installing a lot of new videos and TVs but led to a higher overall depreciation charge.

Janis was taking heed of all the warning signals. Robert was keeping a much more open mind. He made the point that DVR's accounting policies might turn out to be appropriate for a young company which was taking on a vast amount of new business very fast. What the large companies did might be different simply because their business was more mature. He was keen for everyone to agree that if the DVR concept made sense they shouldn't, at that stage, let the problems thrown up by ECI's industry expert dampen their enthusiasm for what he described as a very exciting business.

All the same, Grosvenor started looking at DVR in a different light. Robert described what Brian Hopper had achieved so far as a wonderful springboard for a start up. This meant the risks were considered to be much higher than on first investigation when Grosvenor thought they were being asked to put in lower risk expansion capital*.

Janis was worried that DVR and its advisers weren't presenting the information which Grosvenor needed in a clear and methodical way. As well as the question mark over accounting policies, Janis was finding it difficult to get separate figures for the shops which Brian Hopper intended selling and the direct video rental business which was part of the business that Grosvenor was being asked to invest in.

Robert set out the key issues.

'We need to establish with Brian Hopper that we are not going to be rushed into this deal. We are interested in leading it, but it is more of a start up. There are the problems associated with separating the two shops from the direct

rental side and the accounting policies. **We also need to do further work on how they obtain the level of business. We want to be satisfied that the marketing is right.'**

Thursday, 5 December 1991

Brian Hopper and his advisers, Craig Bonner and Michael Flynn, arrived at Grosvenor for a meeting with Michael Glover and Janis Anderson. This proved to be an exceptionally difficult and frustrating meeting for Brian who was told in no uncertain terms by Michael that he must shed some of his illusions about how much his business was worth.

Craig Bonner had produced some figures which put a value on DVR of £12 million in three years' time if it sold no new contracts and £15 million if it continued to sell 1000 contracts a month. Brian's opening gambit was to suggest that these figures should be used as a basis for working out what DVR was worth now, a suggestion which Michael rejected without argument.

What Grosvenor actually wanted was a much more detailed analysis of DVR's current position and how it intended separating the new direct rental business from the existing shops. Brian found it hard to suppress his irritation. The previous day, he had been round at ECI and had been asked to go through his business plan yet again. Brian was justifiably angry that he was being asked the same basic questions about his business time and time again by different venture capitalists who were meant to be working together, and that at every meeting his advisers were being requested to provide detailed financial breakdowns but always in a slightly different form. Brian wanted the venture capitalists to agree among themselves who was leading so he knew who he was dealing with, but at this point neither Grosvenor nor ECI wanted to put themselves forward as deal leader. But they both saw that it was frustrating for Brian not to know who he was dealing with. It was eventually decided that Grosvenor and ECI would jointly lead the deal, though with Grosvenor doing most of the investigation.

For much of the meeting Michael played the hard man. His clear and unequivocal purpose was to lower Brian Hopper's expectations. Before Candover dropped out of leading the deal it was negotiating to put in £4.4 million for a 20 per cent stake reducing on a ratchet to ten per cent. Michael wanted to make sure that Brian knew that Grosvenor would not be offering anything like this, and that the deal was unlikely to be completed by 20 December.

The thing that Brian remembered most vividly about the meeting was Michael talking about the hole in his balance sheet. There was an argument about the price at which DVR's direct rental contracts should be transferred to the new company. Brian argued that they should be transferred at £200 a set which was roughly the price one of the big rental companies would pay if they were buying the company. Michael argued they would only be worth this if they were actually selling the company, which they weren't.

84

If the contracts were valued at £140 each as proposed, DVR's stake would be worth less than the £4 million which Brian was seeking from Grosvenor, so the shortfall would have to be written into the balance sheet as goodwill and venture capital investors don't like goodwill. Michael pointed out that he would have great difficulty selling a deal to his investors that involved him putting £4 million into a company which the day after the money is invested is only worth, say, £2.8 million. And he warned it will be a problem for the other venture capitalists too.

All this talk of accounting policies was like a red rag to a bull for Brian who felt he had spent much of his working life explaining to accountants and bankers how a rental business works. As he said:

'It's a peculiar business. It's not like a retail business where you buy something for £200 and sell it for £300. In rental you buy something for £200 and the next week you get £8 for it, but that doesn't mean the rental contract isn't worth anything.'

He was also frustrated because he couldn't get people to understand what a fantastic opportunity DVR was.

Looking at it from Grosvenor's point of view, Michael could have said that bluntness at this stage can often save tears and misunderstandings later. There was also the question of Brian's advisers to be clarified. Taking the bull by the horns, Janis asked

Craig straight out, who he was and what financial interest he had in the deal. Grosvenor wanted to know if Craig would benefit financially if the deal went through. Craig called himself a management consultant on a paid retainer from DVR. He confirmed that he would be paid an additional performance fee if the deal went through.

Michael didn't want Brian Hopper to leave with the feeling that all was lost and that somehow Grosvenor were playing some sort of complicated game of cat and mouse with him. He needed to keep Brian sweet and send him away with the nice warm feeling that in spite of everything Grosvenor were nice guys really. He said: 'I believe that you are sitting on a goldmine and that you are doing it right. But I'm an investor and I don't know if this is the right time. Even so, I'm your biggest champion in Grosvenor.'

It did the trick. Brian left the meeting beaming even though he was totally aware that he was being manipulated:

'I'm going to forget all about this meeting apart from the last five minutes. I think Michael really meant what he was saying at the end. I take the view that he was taking up a negotiating stance to try and get me to give up more shares in the company than I am prepared to. He was actually speaking from the heart during those last five minutes.'

Tuesday, 17 December 1991

Grosvenor's offer letter, all eight pages of it, arrived at DVR's office over the fax. Brian Hopper, Eddie Crisp, John Nelson, and Craig Bonner met to try and decipher the deal. For five minutes everyone was absorbed. Craig made detailed notes. When he finished reading he looked up and smiled at Brian. 'At first glance, I think you have got a deal,' he said. Craig's early reaction might have lulled Brian into a false sense of security.

Grosvenor was proposing to invest £4 400 000 in conjunction with ECI and Candover. Most – £4 million – would go in as borrowings to be repaid after four years at the latest. The rest – £400 000 – was to go in as preference shares which would be converted to ordinary shares after four years. The conversion into ordinary shares was to be on a ratchet which would give the venture capitalists between 20 and 50 per cent of DVR depending on how well the company did.

Brian was now intent on pressing for a completion on 15 January. The only stumbling block that he could see was Grosvenor's requirement that he should invest the proceeds from the sale of the two shops into the new business. In fact Brian was pretty cock-a-hoop. Revealing that he hadn't yet got the full grasp of what Grosvenor were proposing he said:

'It's most important to me to get them out on the minimum of equity. I don't mind the interest rates because we can always alter the interest rates by getting different funding and paying them back. The most important thing is that if we do have a company which is worth £200 or £300 million that they walk away with five per cent, or more importantly we have 95 per cent.'

If Grosvenor had been there to see it they would have been relieved to see the modesty of the celebrations. Craig opened a couple of bottles of Muscadet and poured it into plastic cups.

Tuesday, 31 December 1991

Janis got married on the Saturday before Christmas and was now in India on her honeymoon. The job of seeing DVR through to completion had been handed to Lance Phillips. Until yesterday he thought that it was going to be a relatively straightforward process of making sure there was nothing nasty lurking in the accounting policies and steering everyone through the legal loopholes. Little did he know what trouble was in store for him.

The day before it had become clear that Brian Hopper didn't understand the deal which Grosvenor was proposing because either he and his advisers had failed to communicate properly or, as it seemed later on, they didn't feel the offer letter had been clear enough. There were too many people at the previous day's meeting to be able to get to the bottom of Brian's misconceptions, so Lance had decided to use today's visit, which was originally intended as a routine fact-finding tour of one of the distribution warehouses, to get Brian quietly on his own to explain what Grosvenor was looking for and to find out exactly what he wanted too.

However, Lance was not optimistic. He thought there was only a 50 per cent chance that there would still be a deal on the table by Friday – 'It isn't desperately important that this deal goes through. Brian doesn't need to do it. He can continue to grow organically. Grosvenor would like to do it on the right terms, but not at any cost.'

Lance may be a young and inexperienced venture capitalist, but in the few short months which he has been in the business he has developed a distinctive style of his own. He takes an almost fatherly interest in the businessmen he tries to back. He managed to develop a rapport with Brian Hopper which gave Brian the freedom to admit without appearing foolish that he needed help to understand the jargon which surrounds venture capital deals. Lance agreed to work over New Year's Day to get a new deal worked out by Thursday. He wanted Brian to make up his mind one way or the other by Friday.

Brian went away happy, although unsure who to blame for the previous day's debacle – his advisers or Grosvenor:

'I realized I didn't understand the deal. However, I don't think the offer letter was clear. I think we misinterpreted it partly because it was ambiguous. I can see the price of the deal now. Before it was heavily cloaked.'

Thursday, 9 January 1992
At Grosvenor's weekly work-in-progress meeting, Lance explained what went wrong and he was honest enough to place at least some of the blame with the venture capitalists:

'An initial offer from Candover was way off line with what people could agree. Then an offer from ECI which came via us and got changed one more time into a form that nobody was very happy with. It turned out that Brian Hopper didn't even understand it.

'We took a clean piece of paper and started again. The

main stumbling block was that he viewed the IRR just like paying an interest rate. He sat with his calculator and said I'm paying something like an 80 per cent interest rate if things go well and he was unenthusiastic about it, so we scrapped the IRR ratchet.

'We went back to a redemption-type basis which would allow for the three ways in which the company might operate. If it does really badly and they are unable to redeem our loan then we get 51 per cent of the company. If it does fairly well but not outstandingly well then the company will be a cash generator and it can redeem our loan on time and then we will reduce our shareholding from 40 to 30 per cent. We will then have the ability to force the sale of part of the business to get an exit at the end of year five. However, if the company flies and does really well, which I am confident that it will, the company will not be a cash generator. We will not want it to be a cash generator and we have arranged to be able to put in more money if we so desire. We can put in another £5 million before the end of year three, which will take our shareholding back up to 51 per cent again.'

As Robert Drummond explained:

'Brian Hopper now knows there are only two circumstances in which he loses control of his company; either he fails or we put a lot more money in. He either gets the facility to grow the business in the long term or it's a disaster in which case he doesn't deserve to maintain control. So it actually fits his needs very closely which is why it's a good deal.'

'So what could go wrong?' was Bill Edge's parting question. As it transpired, quite a lot.

Monday, 13 January 1992
Brian had accepted the new offer and Grosvenor's investment committee, which on this occasion comprised Robert Drummond, Michael Glover and Bill Edge, met to decide whether this was a deal with which they wanted to continue. Lance who was in

the process of completing his due diligence expected a tough grilling. But it was not as bad as he feared. There were concerns though over new technology. Robert wanted to know if developments such as NICAM stereo and High Definition Television could cause customers to cancel their agreements. Lance was of the view that this was not a significant problem and might in the long run benefit the rental industry. People are more prepared to rent at a time of technological change. They don't want to buy old technology because it will soon be out of date and the new technology is initially too expensive to buy outright.

The question of how you value a rental company had been a running theme both in Grosvenor's internal discussions and in the negotiations with Brian Hopper. Grosvenor was effectively valuing the company at £4 400 000, the amount which the venture capitalists were putting up. Lance reassured the committee that this was a significant discount to the yardstick which the industry usually uses when it values individual TV and video contracts.

The deal got the go ahead subject to still further reassurances on the accounting policies, the appointment of a non-executive chairman, the satisfactory completion of new banking arrangements, and the investigation of DVR's supplier agreements with Akai for the videos and Tatung for the television.

DVR's principal bankers, the Midland, had by this stage indicated their willingness to lend the extra £15 million the company needed to expand the business if the deal with the venture capitalists went through. Brian never lost an opportunity to sing the Midland's praises for the way it had supported his business and he had obviously developed a close working relationship with Philip Mumby who was based at the Midland's corporate banking office in Bedford and who had been DVR's bank manager for the last five years.

But the venture capitalists would only invest if the Midland invested and they would only do so if the accountants gave DVR a clean bill of health and at this stage everyone was still waiting for their report.

Later when it was all over, Brian admitted that he failed to understand the importance of the accountant's report and how much depended on it:

'I didn't treat it seriously enough. I suppose you could say I was feeling rather cocky. I took the view that there was nothing wrong with the business, so they could put in as many accountants and investigators as they liked because they wouldn't find anything wrong.'

Brian is a practical man who likes to get on with running his business and apparently he didn't make any effort to conceal the frustration he felt whenever he had to explain what he saw as the true worth of a rental business to yet another disbelieving accountant. It's a problem which has faced him throughout his twenty years in the TV and video rental business and he just wished he wasn't continually having to go over the same old ground each time he met a new accountant or banker.

Brian's bluntness which in many circumstances stands him in good stead was a bad error of judgement. He needed the trust of the investigating accountant but he made no particular effort to get it. It very nearly cost him the deal. Unfortunately this clash of personalities saw its most damaging reflection in the report the accountants prepared which was far more damning than anyone was expecting.

Thursday, 23 January 1992

The accountants' report had landed on Lance's desk the previous Friday, and Lance had read it with horror. The report questioned certain aspects of the business going back a number of years and cast some doubt on Brian's honesty. Somewhat dismayed Lance made the journey to Dunstable to form his own judgement. As he explained to the work-in-progress meeting:

'When Brian ran and owned the company he did a number of things that he would not be allowed to do if we were investors. He didn't really want to disclose what he had done to the accountants and he let it dribble out as they came across things. I went up to see him and I got the full story of

what had actually gone on over the last eight years. And having heard it I was much relieved because the implication from the accountants was that it could have been a lot nastier than it actually was.

'I think I can understand why he didn't tell us. From the first time we saw him he was saying, look at the business today, look at its potential, forget about what's happened in the past. I think he was lead to believe that we would not want to look at the history. I came away comfortable that what he had done was not a concern to us for the business and he knows absolutely that his position as managing direc- tor of a company in which we are significant investors is completely different from what it has been in the past. I am convinced he is not a rogue.'

As Michael Glover said: 'There was nothing underhand. There was nothing illegal. He acted as though it were a family business which it was and the transactions were not directly involved in DVR or the two shops.'

As far as Grosvenor was concerned that was an end to the matter. If only it had been so simple. In fact the deal continued to trip up on the accountants' report. It was at this point that Candover decided to withdraw from the deal. Instead of looking for a new partner Grosvenor and ECI opted to increase their investment. And it was only thanks to a near superhuman effort from Lance that the deal managed to survive the ripples caused by the accountants' report.

Wednesday, 19 February 1992

The deal was now in the hands of the lawyers, and the slow and nitpicking process of putting the legal flesh on the bones had begun. It's a process which often throws up totally unforeseen problems. In the case of DVR, the traumas of getting the deal this far had been so great that there was an almost palpable collective will to prevent anything from sabotaging it as this late stage. They were still unaware that they were hurtling towards one last obstacle which could derail the whole deal.

It was less than six weeks ago that Lance and Geoffrey Pickerill from solicitors, Lawrence Graham, had sat round a table together. That was when they were both on the same side on Watershed Pictures. This time, Geoffrey Pickerill was representing DVR, and Grosvenor were using Andrew Sheach from Cameron Markby Hewitt.

There were management issues to be sorted out. Eddie Crisp was to become finance director of the new DVR, but Grosvenor, who acknowledged his contribution to date, had expressed some doubts as to whether he had the experience to take on the increased responsibilities which the greatly expanded DVR would bring. Brian Hopper wanted to reward Eddie with a 2.5 per cent equity stake in the company. Grosvenor wanted the decision on Eddie's equity stake to be delayed for six months during which time it would become clear whether or not he had what was needed to take the company on to its next stage of development, but Brian Hopper insisted that this should go forward immediately.

Lance was worried that under present proposals DVR's board was being overloaded with non-executive directors. A non-executive chairman, four non-executive directors as well as the three DVR executives, Brian Hopper, John Nelson, and Eddie Crisp, made for an almost unworkable board. When more than one venture capitalist is involved, there is always the problem of who should go on the board. In this case there were likely to be three venture capitalists, namely Grosvenor, ECI and one other, as yet unknown, since Candover had withdrawn from the deal. In addition, Brian Hopper also wanted his long-standing friend and partner, Graham Littler, on board as a non-executive.

Brian Hopper was unhappy at Lance's suggestion that the board should comprise simply the non-executive chairman and the three executives, with representatives from Grosvenor and ECI present as observers only. Brian was firm that he wanted Graham Littler on the board.

All these detailed negotiations over the fine print, however, would still come to nothing if the bank didn't agree to come up with the loan. And it still hadn't given it the final go ahead. The deal was now waiting on the Midland Bank. Brian Hopper spent

much of the following week on the phone to the bank. Each day
he was promised a decision the following day; each day ended with
no decision being made. The problem was again the accountants'
report. The bank had seen the report and was clearly having second
thoughts. And, although they didn't know this at the time, the top
echelons of the bank must have been already preoccupied with its
negotiations with the Hongkong & Shanghai Bank which led to
the eventual takeover of the bank in July.

However, Brian said he was never in any doubt that the Midland
would finally say yes:

**'The Midland had never turned me down before and I knew
I had a very good case. The loan took so long to come
through because it had to be referred to the regional office
in Reading and then on to head office.'**

Lance was not so sanguine. He thought that the Midland loan was
very much in the balance.

Wednesday, 26 February 1992

Last week Lance realized that this deal was going to fall through
unless some of the sting could be taken out of the accountants'
report and that the bank needed some sort of reassurance from the
accountants that the business really was worth backing.

Lance felt that his career at Grosvenor depended on getting this
deal through. As he said:

**'It is a fairly big deal. It ranks alongside the biggest Grosvenor
has ever done. I also rank alongside the most inexperienced
person Grosvenor has ever had, so if it does fall through there
would be a post mortem which would probably conclude that
they should never have put a kid like me on a deal like this.
The result of which would be that all the slack which I have
been allowed with my pitifully small experience will be reined
in and I'll be kept under somebody's thumb until something
goes right for me. So it is fairly important for me.'**

To understand the unusual nature of the lengths to which Lance
went to push this deal through it is important to realize the status

of these accountants' reports which are commissioned by venture capitalists as part of their due diligence. What accountants are asked to do is present an independent, unbiased account of how they see the business, in this case DVR, both its past history and future prospects. These reports, once written are effectively cast in stone. After all what would be the point of commissioning a report if you could soften its impact whenever you disagreed with its content. But this is what Lance did and the fact that he managed to persuade the accountants to soften the damaging impact of their report was a considerable achievement on his part.

The report concluded that the business was sound and worth backing but much emphasis had been placed on the company's past which gave the report a negative, niggardly feel which Lance felt was wrong. The report left the impression that Brian was untrustworthy, something which Lance felt was both untrue and unfair but on the basis of what had been written he could see that Midland would turn the deal down.

ECI had spent a week trying to persuade the accountants to undo the damage caused by their report, but so far they hadn't budged. In desperation, Brian asked Lance to have a go at changing their mind. The fact that he succeeded where ECI failed is one of the mysteries of this deal.

Lance approached the accountants with the request that the firm should write a letter emphasizing the positive aspects of the company's future and that this covering letter should be sent to the Midland.

To Lance's utter surprise the accountants agreed to do this almost without argument. There followed a nail-biting couple of hours for Lance. He had been sent a fax of the letter which the accountants intended sending, but he had just heard that as the letter stood it was unlikely to give Phil Mumby at the Midland the reassurance he needed. Lance just managed to stop the letter in time. It was being signed and was about to be sent out when Lance phoned.

Having got the accountants to agree to doing a letter in the first place, he was now in the awkward position of having to tell them that the letter needed to be changed. Not knowing what kind of response to expect, he could well have got a flea in his ear, but by this stage Lance had got very little to lose. He rang the partner in charge at the accountants, and boldly asked: 'Before you send this letter will you let me see it and allow me to have my comments factored in?'

Lance had ten minutes to draft his comments. He admitted he didn't actually know what Midland wanted to see. He just knew that the letter as it presently stood which was all about accounting policies wouldn't fit the bill:

'The guy in the Midland wants to have something in his hand that makes him feel warm about DVR again, and no discussion about accounting policies is going to do that. What they have left out of the letter is their comment on the strength of the cash flow which is very attractive and that it is now even better because Brian has been able to knock £10 a set – maybe more – off the price of his supplies.'

The accountants had also asked for a letter from Brian outlining the discussions he was having with his suppliers Akai and Tatung on price. So as well as drafting his own letter Lance phoned Brian at the Castle Hotel in Windsor where he was ensconced with Geoffrey Pickerill in a legal meeting. He told Brian to borrow Geoffrey's laptop computer and get a letter off to the accountants. Lance needed to keep the momentum going; he couldn't afford to let Brian dally over the drafting of this letter so he found himself more or less dictating the contents over the telephone to Brian.

The phone call from the partner at the accountants came through. This was the make or break. Lance fiddled with a paper clip. As he waited and listened he abandoned the paper clip and nervously started drumming his fingers on the desk. The tension was unbearable; time seemed to stand still. Suddenly, a look of total relief spread across Lance's face. 'That's marvellous, that's brilliant, that's excellent, I really appreciate this,' was Lance's response to the accountants' new letter. He was convinced that the new letter would be enough to persuade the Midland. He put the phone down with a look of such triumph and as he did so he punched the air with his clenched fist – a gesture which somehow combined both pleasure and relief.

Lance then telephoned Brian to tell him about the accountants' letter which would say that all the arguments about the accounting policies shouldn't blind people to the fact that DVR had the ability to generate substantial cash flow and profits and that since the accountants reported Brian Hopper had managed to knock another £500 000 from the cost of his supplies.

There was no doubt that this deal was hanging on by its finger tips, and without Lance's determination to persuade the accountants to frame its objections in the context of DVR's ability to generate substantial profits in the future, the Midland Bank would have backed off putting into place the crucial £15 million bank facility and the deal would have failed.

Persuading a venture capitalist to back your business is an emotionally exhausting process. For Brian Hopper it had been a true rite of passage. The point at which he accepted some of the blame for the adverse impression created by the report marked the transition from successful self-made man who can do as he pleases to an entrepreneur with responsibilities and loyalties to more than just himself and his immediate management. Brian now knew that his old 'I've been in this business 20 years and I've been very successful and you can't tell me how to run my business' attitude was no longer appropriate. He had to learn to hold his tongue, and realize that he couldn't turn round to the likes of accountants and tell them, as he did, that he really wasn't fussed what accounting policies they used because their balance sheets were a load of rubbish anyway.

Brian liked the idea of being his own man. Throughout this deal, there had been a part of him which had refused to believe that having a venture capitalist on board was actually any different from just having a bigger overdraft from the bank. At various stages he had talked in terms which indicated that he saw venture capitalists as some sort of necessary evil to be taken advantage of as and when it suited him and discarded at the first possible opportunity.

Lance's bull dog tenacity had undoubtedly won Brian's sympathy:

'I've grown to respect Grosvenor. I do now realize the risks they are taking. Their money goes up on day one and its completely and utterly at risk. They are walking the gang plank with me. In the end it's me and my management team which they are investing in. I didn't realize that three months ago, now I do. I have a better working relationship with them now. There is definitely respect on both sides and I do believe we will work well in the future.'

Wednesday, 11 March 1992

The report from the accountants was still causing waves. Not only had it made the Midland Bank think twice about putting in its £15 million bank overdraft facility, but when the offer finally arrived yesterday it was so hung around with restrictive covenants and conditions that DVR would have found it difficult to meet the targets it had set itself in its business plan. Grosvenor didn't feel able to complete until at least some of the restrictions were relaxed.

Lance spent much of the day negotiating with the Midland and managed to persuade them to give a little on the all important covenants which governed the level of borrowings in relation to profits, assets and cash flow.

Lance spoke to ECI as there were five or six smaller points which he still wanted changed. However, he said he thought Midland had gone as far as they would go, and that they should take a commercial view and complete the deal. Having been thrown in to the depths of despair yesterday, Lance now thought he had broken the back of it. They pencilled in four o'clock tomorrow for completion of the deal. He came off the phone with ECI's agreement and breathed a sigh of relief. With not a touch of irony he said: 'That was a beautiful moment.'

Thursday, 12 March 1992

Nothing had happened to prevent the deal being completed in the afternoon. DVR, Grosvenor and their assorted lawyers and hangers on assembled in the board room of solicitors Cameron Markby Hewitt on Tower Hill. As the afternoon drew on the cars streaming over Tower Bridge on their way home turned to a flicker of red tail lights as darkness fell.

There were still a few details to be sorted out, for example the non-competition letter from Brian's nephew who was buying DVR's two shops in Dunstable and Enfield had not yet been signed. As Lance said there is often a sense of anti-climax about these completion meetings: 'You think it is building up to something and that this is going to be a peak moment, but it isn't. In the end it all sort of seeps into place. The actual signing is never a very dramatic event.'

Michael Glover arrived to sign the agreement for Grosvenor reminding everyone that the last time the BBC filmed a deal being signed, it didn't happen because the bank didn't turn up.

But the Midland did turn up. The bank is often the last piece of the jigsaw to slot into place, and there was a hushed sense of relief as the patrician figure of lawyer, Jeremy Lincoln from the Northampton firm of solicitors Hewitson, Becke & Shaw, who was leading the bank team, entered the room.

A last minute flurry of phone calls and faxes put the finishing touches to the bank's documentation. Biscuits were eaten, fizzy water drunk, fingers tapped the table and Geoffrey Pickerill introduced *Bramble the Cow,* a children's picture book stolen from his three-year-old daughter. In the story Bramble's friend Charlie goes off to work for Old Mr Hopper. Geoffrey inscribed the title page to 'Old Mr Hopper' and sent the book round the table for everyone to sign for Brian.

As if to satisfy Lance's desire for a dramatic moment, Jeremy Lincoln representing the Midland put the phone down on his final call. He turned to the meeting with a sense of urgency which was definitely meant to convey the impression that he held the whip hand and said: 'OK, let's go.'

As usual there was a pile of papers to be got through and a

careful check was made as the signing proceeded to make sure that the right signatures were on all the right bits of paper. Then it was all over. Graham congratulated Brian with a handshake and a 'Well done, mate'. The handshaking continued and the champagne flowed.

Thursday, 30 April 1992

DVR's new non-executive chairman, Robert Chris, held his first board meeting. Lance and Ian Salkeld of ECI were there as observers. As Lance said afterwards, there is this joke among venture capitalists, that the first board meeting is always the worst.

'It's when all the skeletons come out of the cupboard and all the things you didn't find out while you were doing the deal turn up and come as a shock. This one didn't have too many skeletons. There were one or two things, but in the end I didn't even mention them because we were swamped by so much good news that they weren't worth mentioning.

'At the moment, and only six weeks into the investment, the first signs are very positive, the costs look right, the sales look right, and the difference between the two might be very attractive to us. We have to get through the summer which is the slow time of the year for DVR, but if the sales come back at the current rate we could be looking at a further round of investment before too long. At the moment there is no suggestion that they won't meet their target of 200 000 rental contracts by the end of the second year. It is very early to say but the rate at which they are selling now could mean they get up to 500 000 contracts in the foreseeable future.

'During the run up to the investment there were a few hairy moments when I had to put my job on the line over whether Brian Hopper was what he said he was and a lot of people, in fact the majority of people, disagreed with me and as this looks to be an investment which will do well, that is rather satisfying.'

Since the cameras stopped filming, DVR has successfully opened depots to serve the North West and East Midlands as planned. It has gone on to open additional depots covering the West Midlands, the South Wales, Bristol and Swindon areas, and Scotland and Brian Hopper reckons they now cover around 80 per cent of the country. Rentals from these new depots are on budget and it appears that the DVR formula which proved so successful in the South is working well elsewhere, fast fulfilling Brian and his team at DVR's ambition to become number three in the TV and video rental market.

Brian now feels very differently about venture capital than he did in October 1991 when he first embarked upon his search for funds.

'I thought of venture capital as a necessary evil. Selling a stake in my business was simply the means by which I could expand my business fast. I didn't want outside investors for very long; it was always my intention to buy back my business at the first possible opportunity. I don't think that any more. Now I think of it as a partnership. I have found their presence very helpful. Thanks to them we are becoming much more professional and our management and financial reporting is definitely improving.

'I thought they would always be breathing down my neck and looking over my shoulder and I didn't believe them when they said that wasn't their style. In fact I've been pleasantly surprised by their lack of interference. They really have let us get on with the job.'

Chapter Seven

Crossroads

Andrew Slaughter runs an animal funeral business in Hereford-shire where pet owners can have a little funeral and bury their pet in a cemetery dotted around with miniature gravestones to the likes of Tigger, Chad and Sweep. Giving a much loved pet a decent send off is a great comfort to many people when their pet dies. As Andrew explained:

'We provide proper caskets with proper interiors and we lay the pet out just like an undertaker. There is an area where people can come and see their pet before it is buried and we perform a very short non-religious service. Sometimes people bring their whole family. We have had up to 20 people at a dog's funeral.'

Burials are only a small part of Andrew's business which is prin-cipally involved with the disposal by incineration of animal car-casses collected from vets. Andrew runs his incinerator from an outbuilding at his home in Lyonsall in the wilds of the Hereford-shire countryside. It is an extremely profitable business. In 1991 Andrew Slaughter's company, Animal Funeral Services, made a profit of just over £56 000 on sales of £145 100. However, Andrew's business was under threat. His incinerator failed to meet new EC emission regulations, which come into force in October 1995, and it would just not be economic to spend the £100 000 needed to bring his present incinerator up to standard.

Andrew had decided to go for broke. He wanted to buy two huge incinerators and put them on an industrial estate at Droitwich conveniently close to the M5 motorway. This would involve a sixfold jump in his turnover and to fill the incinerators he would have to expand his business into hospital waste, a market which he was only beginning to penetrate.

Andrew had hired professional advisers, Roger Edmunds and Andrew Jameson, of Edmunds Richmond and together they had produced a business plan which had been sent to a number of venture capitalists including Grosvenor where it had landed on Trevor Bayley's desk. It was costing Andrew a fortune in fees; in 1991 it had cost him £20 000; in 1992 it was eating up most of his profits. But if he didn't spend the money he might find himself without a livelihood come October 1995.

Andrew explained how he got into the incineration business.

'It was purely by chance. I was in the exhibition industry working for P & O but the promotion prospects were limited. I thought I'm in a do or die situation. I can either stay and be here for the next 40 years, in the same position, or I can take my chance and work for myself. I think everyone who contemplates going into business for themself must go down the road of looking at pubs, looking at franchises, looking at newsagents. I hit upon this by accident following a chance meeting with someone in the west country. After subsequent research I felt that this was a business which I could put my mark on.

'I like to think I've put the "S" back into service. That might sound terribly corny but if we say we are going to be at a place at a particular time, then we are there. I've proved to the vets that we provide a regular service. That's 365 days a year. We don't stop for holidays, we don't stop for Christmas, we don't stop if it snows. Like the Pony Express – we get through. And that's the way I've built up the business.

'We started with four vets and now we have very nearly 80. We also have a large pet cemetery in Birmingham and another smaller one at my home in Lyonsall.

'We dispose of between 2500 and 3000 animals a month. The work is seasonal. We have got Christmas coming up which is a classic time for people to buy pets. Unfortunately pets get bigger, and when people realize just how much it costs to feed a dog a lot of them end up going to the vets to be put to sleep. It's also true at holiday time. If you have a couple of dogs which have to go into kennels for two or three weeks it puts up the cost of the family holiday. So once again the poor old dog goes to the vet to be put to sleep.

'We have got to the stage where we are at capacity and to meet demand we need to move to a new site. We have also seen a potential in the clinical waste market which is the market we are now really aiming at, although we will still be doing domestic animals and we intend taking on BSE cattle as well.

'Clinical waste is hospital and surgical waste. We have done a survey and at a conservative estimate there are some 300 000 tons of clinical waste a year which need disposing of and the best method of doing this is by incineration.

'We are negotiating on a site at present on an industrial estate at Droitwich which was an old packaging warehouse. The site will be flattened and a new purpose built unit constructed. We are putting in two machines and a further one in about two years' time. A one ton clinical waste incinerator, that is one ton per hour, and a half ton an hour animal carcass incinerator. There will also be cold storage on the site and weighbridges.'

Andrew needed to raise £2.6 million. He had been turned down by a couple of the big clearing banks which was why he was now looking at venture capital.

By the beginning of December 1991, Andrew Slaughter and his business partner, Alaister McLean had already seen two venture capitalists. Alaister was an old friend of Andrew's. He intended giving up his job in the police force to join Andrew's company full time once the finance had been raised. They had yet to see Grosvenor. So far they hadn't formed a particularly favourable impression. Andrew said:

'The problem I've found with venture capitalists is that they will agree to see you, but they haven't really read the business plan which makes me very cross. I can understand they might have 30 separate business plans dropping on to their desk on a Monday morning and to sift through all of these and choose one, two or three must be very difficult. However, I've been really quite upset by the fact that the two venture capitalists I have already seen really haven't bothered to have a good look at the business plan. You can tell by the questions they ask at the interview.

'However, we are still hopeful. One of the problems is that at present we do about 400 tons of animal carcasses a year and we are taking a leap to over 5000 tons. What they don't seem to understand is that the principles remain the same whether you incinerate one ton an hour or one ton a day. In fact it is easier because your handling systems are that much bigger to cope with the greater volume the more you incinerate. The equipment we will be using is very, very high tech. The equipment I use at present is out of the ark and needs constant monitoring. The new equipment is computer controlled.

'If I don't get venture funding, I face closure and the nine people I employ will be out of a job. I feel absolutely terrible because I've put my heart and soul into this. It's taken me a long time to build up the business. In the early days I did everything myself, the driving, the incinerating, the selling and the day-to-day management.'

Thursday, 12 December 1991
Andrew Slaughter, Alaister McLean, and their two advisers, Roger Edmunds and Andrew Jameson, arrived at the Trusthouse Forte Hotel at Heathrow to meet a third venture capitalist. There were Christmas decorations everywhere. The four sat down over coffee in the foyer to plan their approach. They already knew from their previous encounters with venture capitalists that the big jump in turnover proposed in the business plan was posing a problem.

Roger Edmunds hammered home to Andrew that he had a relatively short time to get across the message that the jump in turnover was by no means more than he and Alaister could cope with and that £2.6 million was not too much to invest. Alaister was currently in a job where he controlled 600 people and a budget of £1.5 million and Andrew's business was profitable from the word go. The main risk was that they didn't get enough customers on the clinical waste side. Roger suggested they start talking to the district health authorities. If they could get some letters of intent, or at least near intent, Roger felt this would help their case very much.

Over at the Slough offices of Grosvenor, Bill Edge and Trevor Bayley were meeting ahead of the arrival of Andrew Slaughter and Alaister McLean and their two advisers. Trevor's initial reaction to the business plan was not promising:

'It gives a good analysis of the market and the competition and there is a reasonable description of the business and how they intend to move forward. Unfortunately there are a whole load of appendices which they haven't sent us which put flesh on the bones. They have given some numbers which don't look too promising. This is probably a slightly marginal deal at this point, but it is certainly worth talking to them. The profit projections they have put in don't seem to justify the level of investment they are looking for. They are talking in terms of raising £2.6 million and only making profits at a respectable level in years three or four. Given these numbers it is difficult to see how we could get a satisfactory return.'

So as the meeting began it didn't look good for Andrew and his partner Alaister. Trevor thanked everyone for making the trek to sunny Slough and started by sketching in Grosvenor's background and the kind of deals it was currently doing. Andrew explained how he came to start the business and how he operated.

It was only then that the penny dropped with Bill Edge and he realized just how important the deal was to Andrew and that without it he didn't have a business at all after October 1995.

Bill was extremely interested in the nuts and bolts of how the business would run. Could they still operate with one driver? How did they intend moving and lifting the heavier animals? And how did they expect to run the place hygienically? This gave Andrew the opportunity to display the depth of his technical knowledge. Andrew was convinced that much of the competition still hadn't woken up to the fact that many of the incinerators now operating would be illegal after October 1995. Nor was he convinced that the manufacturers had got it right either. There had been occasions when Andrew had asked manufacturers for their test results and these had not been forthcoming.

Andrew was working with a manufacturer in Durham, Silent Glow. The machines he wanted to buy were based on a German design and while the plant was being built he intended working closely with the manufacturer and Her Majesty's Inspectorate of Pollution which was responsible for granting the licence.

Just like all the other venture capitalists who Andrew and Alaister had seen, Bill was concerned that they might not pick up enough contracts for clinical waste. As he said the Government was very good at imposing rules, such as all clinical waste should be burned, but it didn't then provide funds to pay for it. Andrew sought to reassure them with the statistic that as his proposed incinerator would only burn up to 10 000 tons of clinical waste a year he was only trying to capture three per cent of the total market.

Roger Edmunds outlined the financial deal which they were looking for. The company needed to raise £2.6 million. The land would cost £750 000, the building £450 000, ancillary expenses £170 000 and there was £600 000 for working capital. They were proposing two sorts of ordinary shares: A shares for the founder shareholders, and B shares for the outside investors. Between £1.3 and £1.4 million was to go in as redeemable preference shares repaid in year five; £750 000 as a long-term loan secured on the fixed assets repaid at the end of year four, and £500 000 as an overdraft repaid at the end of year two. The projections assumed that a third incinerator would be installed in year three out of the company's own resources and that the company itself would be sold on at the end of year five.

Bill was still worried that they wouldn't get enough orders for clinical waste. As he said unless the orders came in quickly during the first year there would be a dreadful cash drain on the company.

He said from bitter experience that companies were often too optimistic at the beginning; the orders did usually come in but they came in a lot slower than anticipated.

Andrew had already applied for planning permission and the application would be heard at the end of January. He wanted to be in a position to buy the site as soon as the permission came through. At that stage he didn't envisage any difficulty getting planning permission. His discussions with both the district and county councils had given no hint of the difficulties and frustrations which he would eventually meet.

The local council had been worried by the potential smell. To get over this Andrew had agreed to install a refrigerated animal store. There had been some articles in the local newspapers and he had been on the local radio a couple of times, but he hadn't heard of any opposition to his proposal, only curiosity. His site was hidden from view by a giant Kays warehouse and the prevailing wind was in the opposite direction from the nearest residential area, a housing estate a quarter of a mile away.

After the meeting Trevor owned up to his initial prejudice; before meeting Andrew he had found it difficult to be dispassionate about the proposal, and he was worried as to whether other people at Grosvenor might find the whole idea distasteful. However, Bill and Trevor both agreed that they had been impressed by Andrew and his advisers. Bill asked Trevor to work out what kind of rate of return they could expect. It was Bill's view that if it came out at 20 or 30 per cent a year, it wasn't worth the risk, but if it came out at 50 or 60 per cent then it looked good.

Thursday, 19 December 1991

Trevor brought the proposal to the weekly work-in-progress meeting. Janis Anderson asked if Andrew really was Mr Slaughter. This was the joke which had been doing the rounds in the office. Trevor had been expecting some ribaldry and was not very surprised when he got it. Janis Anderson who was getting married the following week was obviously demob happy. Trevor chose to ignore the nudge, nudge, wink, wink atmosphere round the table. He ploughed on regardless admitting to his own initial scepticism.

As Robert Drummond said: 'First of all you laugh, but when you think about it, it must take off.'

Friday, 10 January 1992

A typical Herefordshire cottage, plain, double fronted with a canopied porch, whitewashed stone with black woodwork under a slate roof. Two large executive cars swept down the icy country lane, the first missed the gateway, turned back and entered the yard to be greeted by a bouncy golden retriever. This was Litfield House, Andrew Slaughter's home. Beside the house were the outbuildings which contained the incinerator. In the yard there were the two vans which did the pick ups from the vets and some brand new stables.

Trevor Bayley and Stephen Edwards from Grosvenor had come out to Lyonsall to see Andrew's business in operation. Grosvenor were the first venture capitalists to visit. Even though his operation was extremely profitable Andrew was worried that his visitors might be expecting something much grander and more impressive. There was nothing much to see except what was effectively just a very large oven in a farm outbuilding.

The party which also included Andrew's advisers, Roger Edmunds and Andrew Jameson, began with a visit to the incinerator. From the outside it looked just like any other country cottage with outbuildings. A discreet chimney emitting nothing more than a heat haze and a slight roar was the only clue to the activity which was taking place in Andrew's outbuilding. Andrew had not had one single complaint about the incinerator in the four and a half years he had been here. It might have been better if he had. It would have given him some idea of the opposition he was to encounter later from the planning authorities.

Inside Andrew demonstrated the controls. It was a cold day outside, but when Tony Talbot who was operating the incinerator opened the door, a wall of heat hit them and the deep red glow of the furnace fire seemed to plunge the rest of the room into darkness.

Andrew's office was a small room in his house with a desk and a computer. He didn't need anything larger or grander to run his business, so today's meeting was taking place in the family sitting room round a large wood burning stove with Syd, the ginger and white cat, curled up asleep on the back of the sofa behind Trevor's head.

It was planned to transfer Andrew's present company Animal Funeral Services into a new company, Crossroads, once agreement had been reached to build the new incinerators. The draft accounts for Animal Funeral Services arrived yesterday and Trevor was keen to go through them line by line. Once exceptional expenses such as advisers' fees and work to the house were deducted, Trevor could see that the company had a strong cash flow.

Grosvenor were going to need a lot of reassurance that Andrew would be able to attract enough contracts for clinical waste to make the incinerator pay. Andrew was convinced that the hospitals wanted someone to take their incineration problem off their hands. He suspected that those which currently did their own incineration might not be in a financial position to replace their existing incinerators before the new regulations come in to force in 1995. They had also been contacted by a contractor who wanted to use all the new incinerator's capacity. Putting all their eggs in one basket like this was not something which Andrew wanted to do, but it did indicate that the demand was out there.

Michael Glover at Grosvenor had asked Trevor to raise the question of whether or not Andrew's new incinerator might attract government grants. The siting of the incinerator near a motorway seemed to be Andrew's prime consideration. The preferred site at Droitwich was not in a development area which made it unlikely that any grants would be available. They were also looking at another site near Bilston where there might be the possibility of grants. The idea of pursuing government grants was not greeted with much enthusiasm. Roger Edmunds said they wanted to make sure the figures stacked up without them, while Andrew Jameson warned of the dangers of getting bogged down in bureaucracy and losing the initiative if they went down the route of seeking government assistance.

Lunch was Hawaiian chicken and baked potatoes which Andrew had cooked himself. Once the dishes were cleared away, they made arrangements for driving to Droitwich to see the proposed incinerator site. Trevor wanted a reaction to Grosvenor's intention to appoint a non-executive chairman. He also felt that the new company would need to improve its financial and accounting systems. Alaister said they had expected that Grosvenor would want to put in a non-executive chairman. However, Roger Edmunds said the new company would not need a full time financial director and that his firm intended supervising the financial side of the business on the basis of two days a month. Trevor was not certain that that would be sufficient. However, he was impressed by the suggestion that Alistair Carroll of Silent Glow, the incinerator manufacturer, should join the board as a non-executive technical director.

As Trevor and Stephen drove to Droitwich it became clear that Trevor was still undecided. His gut feeling was that the deal should be rejected; although he acknowledged that somebody could make a lot of money out of it. He was also concerned as to whether Andrew was up to managing a larger company. And there was the problem of syndication. This was not a deal which Grosvenor would want to do on its own, and it wouldn't be a deal which would be easy to sell to other venture capitalists.

Thursday, 16 January 1992

Andrew had now run into problems with the planning permission for the Droitwich site. The clinical waste incinerator which Andrew intended building would be the first of its kind in this country and yet the district council was now saying that it wanted to see a similar incinerator in operation before it was prepared to give planning permission.

Trevor wanted to keep Crossroads on Grosvenor's list of possible deals so he had decided to present the proposal in a relatively positive light at today's work-in-progress meeting. He pointed out that Andrew had spotted a lucrative market for clinical waste incineration where contracts were typically signed for eight to ten years and where gross margins were as high as 80 per cent.

Trevor was impressed with Andrew's achievements and his ability and knowledge of the industry. However, the management team was inexperienced, but Trevor had been reassured that the operation of a large incinerator was not much different from that of a small one. Trevor was still worried that the deal would be difficult to syndicate. Andrew was talking to other venture capitalists and Trevor wanted to be free to encourage him in the hopes that another venture capital partner might emerge.

Trevor thought highly of Roger Edmunds, and the work he had done on the deal. Roger was hoping that Trevor might have good news for him today. Trevor let him down gently with the news that while Grosvenor were interested in proceeding, he was not doing any more work on the deal until the planning permission had been sorted out. But he by no means slammed the door on the deal. He told Roger that Grosvenor might be interested in funding half the deal if Crossroads could find another venture capitalist.

Wednesday, 26 February 1992

It was looking less and less likely that Crossroads was going to get planning permission for the Droitwich site. Even so Trevor had decided to accompany Andrew and Alaister to the Wasteman exhibition at the National Exhibition Centre in Birmingham. This was a major industry exhibition and as it is held only once a year, it was a good chance for Trevor to learn more about the industry in the event that Grosvenor did the deal.

But as Trevor said it was looking increasingly unlikely:

'The critical point for us is the state of the planning permission. It has been turned down at district level. It's gone to Hereford and Worcester County Council who are stalling. The next hearing is 12 March, but the council have said it may not go before the committee until April and it may even be delayed until June. Andrew feels the council is scared to make a decision. They don't really have a valid reason for turning it down on planning grounds which is what they would like to do. It's the NIMBY phenomenon – Not In My Back Yard. The council appreciate the need for a waste incinerator, but they would rather that the next Council along did it.

'If the County Council does turn it down Crossroads will

have to appeal to the Department of the Environment. The national government can't avoid the issue by shoving it onto the nearest council. If Andrew doesn't get a decision on 12 March they do have an alternative site and they are going to lodge a planning application for that site too.

'I think Andrew still has a long way to go particularly with the planning permission. There is no way we can even vaguely commit ourselves until we know where they are going to be. It's a chicken and egg situation. They have probably been too early going for finance, but having said that there is no point in getting a site and making an offer on it if they don't know they have the finance in place, so they are caught in a difficult situation, and I suspect from our point of view nothing will happen now for the next five or six months.'

Andrew was finding the planning problems extremely frustrating. He was now reconciled to the fact that the county council was unlikely to give the scheme the go ahead without a fight and that an appeal to the Department of the Environment was a virtual certainty. As he said: 'The county council want the DOE to make the decision for them, so they can turn round and say it isn't us who are the bad guys, it's the DOE.'

But Andrew was also frustrated with the venture capitalists. He would have liked them to commit themselves ahead of the planning permission, so if and when it finally did come through he could move quickly because all the paperwork would be completed. His view of venture capitalists was that they are a nervous bunch. He said:

'It confirms my feeling that this country is run by accountants and not by managers. We have been to about 30 venture capitalists and we have only managed to hook two of these. People have said we are too small, others have said we are taking too much of a jump. Grosvenor are taking more interest than most, but they are still going very softly, softly.

'I feel I'm very much in the doldrums at present. Not actually living my life on the edge but very close to it. I believe a lot in this business, I believe that I can make money both for myself and the investors.'

Thursday, 12 March 1992

Trevor was convinced that Andrew wouldn't get planning permission at today's meeting of the Hereford and Worcester County Council's planning committee. He had decided to tell Grosvenor's regular Thursday work-in-progress meeting to take Crossroads off the list of possible deals. Grosvenor had a well developed system for rejecting deals. If a deal was DW – dead withdrawn – as was the case with Crossroads, there was still the possibility that the deal could be brought back at some later date. However, if a deal was DR – dead rejected – this meant that Grosvenor had decided against backing it and it wouldn't be resuscitated. A Midlands firm of venture capitalists had also expressed interest in Crossroads, and as Trevor didn't want to slam the door entirely on the deal he intended telling Andrew to carry on talking to the other venture capitalist and to come back to Grosvenor when he got planning permission.

It was unlikely that the planning appeal would be heard much before the end of the year; he might give Andrew a ring then to find out how it went. On the other hand he might well be in the thick of something else.

At the end of June, Trevor was surprised to get a call from Roger Edmunds requesting another meeting. Roger and Andrew had been working on an alternative way forward for Crossroads which didn't depend on getting immediate planning permission. Could they come and discuss their ideas with Trevor?

Wednesday, 1 July 1992

Roger and Andrew arrived at Grosvenor. Andrew had been out on the road driving the van. Dressed in jeans and an open neck black and red check shirt, he looked very different from the normal run of sobre-suited businessmen who pass through Grosvenor's reception room daily. As Trevor took them through to the meeting room, Andrew apologised for his appearance and Trevor joked that some of us have to work for our living.

Roger produced a short agenda for the meeting. Trevor was brought up to date on the state of the planning permission. The news was worse than expected. Hereford and Worcester had refused to give planning permission. Andrew hoped the appeal would be by written evidence, but he had now heard that the County wanted a public enquiry. The appeal which was to start at the end of November would last for two weeks. Andrew was determined to fight on but he was now at a distinct disadvantage as he couldn't afford to be legally represented. He had also been told that it could be another eighteen months before a decision was actually announced.

Attempts to find other sites had met with similar problems. A leasehold site at Hartlebury looked promising, until the landlord suddenly changed his mind about letting to Crossroads. This was not encouraging news. Trevor was initially so enthusiastic about Crossroads because Andrew had spotted a hole in the market and he seemed to be ahead of the competition. If he was going to have to wait two years for planning permission he was unlikely to be in such a favourable position.

As Roger said: 'If we are going to be stopped by the bureaucrats we have to look at other ways of developing the business.' It was these alternative plans which Roger and Andrew now wanted Grosvenor to back.

Andrew was in the process of buying Petorium, a similar business to his own serving 51 vets along the M4 corridor. Andrew was basically buying Petorium's customer base, taking Animal Funeral Services to number three position in the country. There was no plant and equipment coming with the deal as all of the incineration could be dealt with at Lyonsall.

It was also the reason why Andrew was out on the road driving the van today. He was in the process of visiting his new vets, to find out their needs and to forge the kind of links which helped cement his reputation for service.

But it was not the Petorium deal which was the real reason behind today's visit to Grosvenor – Andrew could fund that from his own resources.

Andrew had learnt that a rival company in the veterinary disposal business already had a licence to burn clinical waste at its incinerator near Rugby and the company was for sale. Andrew had already told the owner that he was interested in buying the business, and he wanted Grosvenor to back him.

The proposal was in two parts. The first part involved expanding the animal disposal business. If he acquired the rival company he intended moving his operations to Rugby near junction 18 on the M1. There was an adjacent farm house which was currently rented out but which the owner had indicated might be for sale as well.

The business was on sale for a quarter of a million pounds which Andrew argued could be a better deal than the Droitwich site which would have cost £700 000 before it even produced a penny of income. Andrew did acknowledge that there were problems with the company. Most pet disposal businesses charge on a per animal basis, so a cat is charged at one price, a small dog at another, and a large dog at yet another. The other company charged per bag regardless of how many animals there were in the bag. Andrew wanted to change this company's charging structure and at the moment he couldn't say how much resistance he would meet from the vets. He thought not much because the extra charge would simply be passed on to the customer.

As well as becoming number three in the pet disposal business, Andrew was particularly interested in the other company's clinical waste disposal licence. This would give him a valuable first foothold in the market which he had identified as having so much potential.

Andrew was going ahead with the Petorium deal come what may. However, if he was to get this other company as well, it made sense to include the Petorium acquisition in his bid for outside funding. Roger and Andrew had worked out that the two deals will cost a total of £1.9 million over 18 months and that they were looking to raise around £1.8 million. The figures, excluding the lease on the farm house, included £750 000 to buy the company; £200 000 for Petorium; £104 000 to refurbish the house and £340 000 for a new half-a-ton-an-hour incinerator.

The second stage of the deal was to go ahead with the original proposal to get into the clinical waste market on a separate site in year three once all the planning hurdles had been crossed. Andrew then proposed to buy a second incinerator capable of burning clinical waste at the rate of two tons per hour. The price had significantly increased from his first proposals. A two-ton incinerator, equipped to treat waste water and ash, which would close down within 20 seconds if permitted emission levels were exceeded would cost £3.5 million and take a year to build.

Andrew had been talking to a major water company about the possibility of a joint venture once Andrew had got planning permission. Andrew had been reassured by the water company's own research which indicated that the clinical waste market was larger than the 300 000 tons a year which was generally bandied about within the industry.

From Trevor's point of view, Andrew and Roger's new proposal presented several problems; it was more ambitious, it would cost more and it lacked the simplicity and clarity of purpose that the first proposal had. Trevor also disliked the fact that the farmhouse on the site where Andrew would live formed part of the deal. Roger met this point immediately saying they would be prepared to structure the deal without the house.

The meeting finished with Trevor warning Andrew and Roger that Grosvenor was in the process of raising extra money from investors and until this was forthcoming later on in the year, every deal was being very carefully scrutinized.

Trevor was in two minds:

'I think it is an interesting proposal. It's well thought through and I continue to be extremely impressed by Roger Edmunds. I think his role in the company is critical, not only from the point of view of the relationship with us as potential investors but also to introduce disciplines to the business. Andrew I like as well. He has a good sense of humour and for a sole proprietor he has got quite a good strategic awareness of where he wants his business to go. So there are a lot of positive things.

'On the negative side it was always going to be a difficult one to sell internally and if anything it will probably be more difficult rather than less difficult. I'm unwilling to reject

something if I believe in it just because it is difficult to sell, but I need to think more about it. It is still a huge step for the company and it will be an extremely high risk investment for us to make, although probably less high risk than to build the facility from scratch as they were talking about before. Roger has done very detailed financial projections, but there are a few fundamental questions which need to be answered.

Thursday, 2 July 1992
It took Trevor less than a day to make up his mind. He had decided to reject the new deal because it failed to exploit the hole in the market created by the new EC regulations which was the attraction of Crossroads' first proposal. In Grosvenorspeak this deal was now DR which was what he recommended at today's work-in-progress meeting. He explained the new proposals in the briefest detail and no one questioned his decision.

117

Andrew had come to accept that incineration was a business which had got a bad name and that this was going to make it very difficult for him to raise the money effectively to save his business and save his livelihood.

'We are downhearted but not suicidal. I can't stand still because this is my business and I like what I do and I want to see it succeed. I've still got this urge to go forward. My goal is to install a two-ton clinical waste incinerator and a half-ton veterinary waste incinerator. But if I can't get that I might decide that I've done my best. If I sold up I would find another niche business. I'm not finished yet. At least I had a go.'

In the middle of November 1992 Andrew finally admitted that bureaucracy had got the better of him. His planning consultant warned him that he didn't stand a chance of winning the public enquiry on the Droitwich site unless he commissioned a full environmental impact survey at a cost of £15 000. Andrew no longer had that sort of money available and so he decided to withdraw his planning application.

Andrew was now carefully considering his options: whether to sell his business, or continue to look for ways to expand but on a smaller scale. He still had plenty of options open to him. He could carry on running his incinerator at Lyonsall for the next couple of years, replacing it with a new model when the new EC regulations come into force in October 1995. He had also found an alternative site, four miles away, where the local landowner might be willing to do a joint venture with him.

The experience of the previous two years had left Andrew with the feeling that there ought to be a better way of financing small businesses like his.

'Over the previous three years, I have invested around £60 000 in fees to various advisers, and at the end of the day I have nothing to show for it. So far not one of the banks, venture capitalists or potential joint venture partners has offered to put their hand in their pocket to help me finance the work needed to get planning permission. People have told me I have foresight, I have vision but without planning permission I can't even get started. I am reluctantly coming to the view that getting into the big time in the incineration business is beyond the resources of a small business and that in the end it will be the big corporations who can afford to hire the best lawyers and the best planners who will make all the money out of the new era of incineration which begins when the new EC regulations come in to force in October 1995.'

Chapter Eight

Pharmaceutical Proteins Limited

Biotechnology companies are high risk investments even by the standards of venture capital. Biotechnology is by its very nature a highly speculative activity and the venture capitalists who back an early stage biotech company may not know for many years whether or not the line of research being pursued by their scientists is capable of commercial exploitation.

Pharmaceutical Proteins Limited (PPL) is a British biotech company which breeds sheep to produce certain special proteins in their milk. If these proteins prove successful in clinical trials they could be used in the treatment of haemophiliacs and in lung diseases such as emphasaema. There are possible nutritional uses too.

PPL had successfully produced a number of sheep which had been genetically modified to produce one of two proteins, Alpha I Antitrypsin (AAT) or Factor IX. Tracey, PPL's first genetically modified or transgenic sheep, became something of a media star during the summer of 1991 when it became known that quantities of AAT were present in her milk.

PPL was formed in 1986 to commercialize the work of the Institute of Animal Physiology and Genetics Research, a government research institute. It was initially funded by two venture capitalists; Prudential Venture Managers and Transatlantic Capital and the government agency, Scottish Enterprise.

Grosvenor first became involved when PPL did its third round of fund raising in May 1990 investing £500 000 at £3 a share. That was at the point in PPL's development when it had become clear that the scientists had managed to produce sheep which had been successfully genetically modified to contain the AAT-producing gene and the management had been strengthened. Grosvenor's investments in high technology and biotechnology companies are normally made at the stage of a company's development when the research is shown to be capable of being commercially exploited.

At Grosvenor, PPL is looked after by Janis Anderson, who finds the company's work fascinating. But this was not so much a story about doing good science, which is how PPL's managing director Ron James described what the company hopes to achieve with one of its newly signed long-term research contracts; but rather more about the different aims and objectives of the various investors. Differences which the scientists who are working in biotech companies like PPL often feel have little to do with their actual work.

PPL found itself in the fortunate position of being offered significantly more money than it set out to raise. Should they take all the money on the basis that a 'bird in the hand . . .'; or should they turn some of it away, and take it later when the company would be worth more and the shares could be sold at a higher price? If lots of shares were sold at a low price, some investors might have to accept that their stake in the company would be diluted.

Or should they sell fewer shares even though there was a risk that when they next wanted the money, biotechnology might be out of fashion, and the money more difficult to raise? Or should they sell the shares at a higher price and run the risk of not raising as much money? These were the questions which the venture capitalists had to resolve.

PPL's research is based around sheep and the disadvantage of working with sheep is that they take nearly a year from conception to become sexually mature. This, and the need to maintain a small farm and a flock of 600 specially imported scrapie-free New Zealand sheep, means that the work is time consuming and expensive. For these reasons much of the initial experimental work was undertaken with mice and only if successful was it then transferred to sheep.

By the end of 1991, the company was sufficiently confident in its technology to attract two large commercial partners: Bayer, the

German drug company, and the American nutritional company, Wyeth Ayerst, and several smaller contracts. Revenues from these contracts were not sufficient to fund PPL's entire work and in any case PPL's investors were also keen for the company to develop its own drugs because the company would only ever become really valuable if it exploited its own discoveries.

It was always planned that the company would go for a fourth round of funding in the spring of 1992, when it should be able to demonstrate that an improved gene which had worked well in mice had been successfully incorporated into a new generation of transgenic sheep. However, PPL started running out of money before then and in early November 1991 some of the existing investors, including Grosvenor, put in an additional £900 000 of loan capital to be converted into shares at the time of the next financing.

PPL's managing director, Ron James, took up the story at the beginning of 1992:

'When we went out to seek new investors, the first place we looked was among UK investors and we did get some interest from the small number of real venture capitalists which are left in the UK industry, but it really wasn't sustained and it wasn't all that enthusiastic and, at the end of the day, we had no concrete offers.

'At that time there was a lot of interest in biotechnology stocks in the USA. They were all gaining in value on their stock market and one of our investors, APAX, had a US associate, Patricoff & Co, who we went to see. Patricoff had already made an investment in another transgenic company called DNX so they understood the technology. They really only had to assess our management and our markets and they liked what they saw. They then helped us find another US venture capitalist, Hancock Ventures. This second US venture capitalist introduced us to a French venture capital fund, Sofinnova, and they too decided to invest.

'The interesting thing is we set out to raise about £3 million and the new investors from the USA and France between them decided to offer us £4 million. When that happened I think our own existing investors realized that may be the company they had was worth something. The UK venture capitalists then suddenly got quite enthusiastic about putting more money in too. We are now in the delightful position of being offered somewhere close to £7 million when we set out to find £3 million.

'The management problem which results from this is how do you justify taking in the extra money and can you get a good return on the extra money which is being offered you? Or should you turn away some of that money and raise it later when you need it at a higher valuation?

'The venture capital theory is that you shouldn't take it, you should wait until you get a higher valuation. However, they all know that raising money is difficult and when it's offered they may turn away from the theory and say – or most of them will say – grab what you can get.'

Ron James is a gamekeeper turned poacher so he could see the issues from both the company's and the investors' points of view. He used to work for Prudential Venture Managers, the venture capital arm of the Prudential Corporation, one of PPL's original investors. He put himself up for the job of managing director two years ago when the previous incumbent left. He said it had been the most exciting and stimulating two years of his life.

It also meant that although he understood the dilemma which faced the investors, particularly Grosvenor; it was the company, its future and its employees which were now his main priority and an additional £7 million would give him a lot of freedom to manoeuvre. PPL was at the stage where it could usefully consider merging with one or more companies operating on similar projects.

Ron James continued:

'Our thinking about mergers originated when we were looking for a way of getting a flotation on the US market. One of the problems of venture capital investment in the UK is that there is no easy exit. The UK Stock Exchange is only interested in companies which are at a much more advanced stage and making profits. In the US, high tech companies can get a stock market listing while they are still very much at the research stage.

'When we realized that, in theory, a UK company could get access to the US market, the question then became how to do it in practice. The only way you can sell a UK company to US investors is to have a strong US influence. We already had predominately US customers. The next thing to go for was US investors and then perhaps a US partner. We started to look at companies that we might be able to join with. At the same time some of our competitors approached us and suggested that we might like to merge with them. It's now a question of carefully evaluating the options and deciding which if any we go for and the order in which we do them.'

It was the middle of May and the time was fast approaching when Grosvenor had to decide whether or not it would join in this round of funding. Janis had recently returned from the company's annual general meeting where she discovered that only Prudential was prepared to go along with Grosvenor and voice its concerns over the price and size of the new issue of shares. Prudential didn't intend investing in this round and was concerned about having its shareholding diluted by a large influx of new shares issued at too low a price.

Janis reported her findings to the weekly work-in-progress meeting. She had quite uncharacteristically locked her PPL papers in her briefcase and mislaid the combination. Her colleagues treated this outbreak of scattiness with indulgent good humour. Speaking without the benefit of her papers Janis explained that the new issue appeared to be around £6.8 million which included funds from two new US investors Patricoff & Co and Hancock Ventures and two new French investors APAX Paris and Sofinnova.

APAX London is a venture capitalist which specializes in high tech investments and which invested in PPL at its second round of financing when the company raised £1.2 million in 1989. APAX London, Patricoff & Co in the US, and APAX Paris, although entirely separate firms with their own boards of directors, are loosely associated. It was a concern at Grosvenor that after this fourth round of fundraising these three venture capitalists would end up with 40 per cent of the company.

The price of the new issue was 375p. Robert Drummond was worried that the price was too low. The price was only just over 20 per cent ahead of the previous year's fundraising at 300p and as he said: 'The company has passed a lot of milestones since then. So either we overpaid a year ago or the price is too low. If you tell me that 375p a share is all this business is worth and we shouldn't increase our stake then I'll live with it but I'm not prepared to accept it at this stage.'

Robert was surprised when Janis told him that the other shareholders appeared to take the view that the company should take in as much money as they could at this round and that the price should be 375p.

Robert wondered if he was over reacting which gave Janis the chance to put PPL's case for taking the money. As she said the company was still not totally secure and if it was to move forward it would have to merge with a US company.

Later, when Robert and Janis met quietly together he took Janis's point that if the price was low that might be what was needed to bring in the US investors which in itself was likely to put the company in a much stronger position to make mergers and eventually seek a quote on the US stock exchange.

Hamish Hale at APAX occupied a pivotal position in this deal. Robert and Janis agreed that it would be useful if they met him privately to voice their concerns and a meeting was fixed for the end of May at Grosvenor's offices in Slough.

Surprisingly, Robert didn't use the occasion to confront Hamish head-on over the issue of the price. The two men did a polite but wary dance around each other, beginning with inconsequential chat about the state of their respective businesses. Hamish must have been aware of Robert's concerns. However, they were referred to only very obliquely during the meeting which Robert used to probe APAX's thinking on PPL.

Hamish made it clear to Robert that he didn't consider the

amount which PPL was raising to be excessive when compared to the amounts which some other biotechnology companies had raised. He said it would enable the company to develop its own intellectual property rather than become principally a company which did research and manufacturing under contract to other organizations. He described it as PPL's war chest which would allow it to get on with running the company rather than having continually to squander its energies on raising fresh funds.

By the end of the meeting Robert had a much better idea of how APAX was thinking but he still remained to be convinced that the price was right. He said, 'APAX has a very good argument for the company needing the money. The problem still is that it is being raised on terms which are not very attractive to us and I suppose we are now at the stage where we could sound out one or two of the other shareholders to see how they feel about it.'

During the meeting Janis revealed that the new shareholders had noticed that there were rights attaching to an earlier class of shares which they wanted removed. When Grosvenor first invested in May 1990, one of the other venture capitalists who came in at the same time had insisted that the shares issued at that time had the right to extra shares if PPL failed to achieve a certain growth rate. It was this liability to create an unknown number of shares at some point in the future to which the new investors were objecting.

Janis was not on the board of PPL but she did attend board meetings as an observer from time to time. In early June, the company held its first board meeting for two months at Trans-atlantic Capital's offices in London's Marylebone Road. PPL was already in merger talks with a number of companies. However, the likely future shape and direction of the company had yet to emerge. As the need to do a merger in the US was one of the principal reasons why PPL had decided to raise so much money at this stage, Janis once again raised Grosvenor's concerns about the size and price of this current round of fundraising. Over the previous couple of weeks Janis had spoken to a number of PPL's investors, some of whom had said they shared Grosvenor's concerns. However, with the exception of Prudential, none were prepared to voice their worries at the meeting and she was now unlikely to win over any of the other investors.

Most of the investors appeared to take the view that the large amount of money being raised may have driven down the price, but it seemed to be accepted that if this removed the company from the burden of constantly thinking about how and where the next tranche of money was coming from, then this might be a price worth paying.

The contrary view was that companies with too much money tend to spend it, and that companies like PPL should only have enough money for their immediate needs. And while Janis was sure Ron James would keep PPL on a tight financial rein, the idea that PPL might end up with more than double what it set out to raise, did cause Janis some anxiety.

For the first time Janis indicated that Grosvenor might well decline to put in any extra money at this stage unless it knew where the money was going. Ron James promised that a revised business plan would be available seven days before the closing date for the offer on 30 June 1992.

There were now less than three weeks before the offer closed on PPL's fourth round of fundraising. Janis brought the weekly work-in-progress meeting up to date. The impression she had gained from the last board meeting was that the other shareholders were happy to sell the new shares at 375p if this was the price which would bring in the US investors and make it easier to get a US stock market listing at some point in the future.

In the period since the board meeting, PPL had received an offer of around £4 a share from a quoted US company working in a similar field. Janis and the other shareholders took the view that unless this company could come up with a better offer, it would be preferable for PPL to go ahead with its own fundraising.

Robert worried that possibly PPL hadn't done enough to get the best offer for the purchase of the company. Janis explained that at this stage of PPL's development there were probably only a limited number of companies which would be interested in bidding for it.

By the end of June, when the fundraising finally went through, PPL had still not persuaded Grosvenor to invest in this round.

However, Janis had skillfully renegotiated the rights attached to the earlier shares. These rights were dropped in exchange for warrants to buy shares at 375p at some time in the future. This satisfied the new shareholders who now knew exactly how many new shares would be issued; and it satisfied Grosvenor who could now come back at a later stage and buy shares at 375p, the same price as the current round of fundraising.

As Ron James said with no small hint of admiration:

'We were unable to convince Janis that we needed more than the £5 million and we had £5 million without Janis's investment. She was quite clever, because she got the incoming investors to agree to increase the warrants on the conversion of the old shares, so she will be able to buy in later for the same price and I think that is probably what she intends to do.'

Janis explained:

'I decided against investing for a whole range of reasons, some of which had more weight than others. But, in principle, I felt that there were sufficient funds coming in from third party investors and some existing investors, so our lack of further investment wouldn't necessarily influence the success of the business. The amount we had remaining to invest in this sector and specifically in PPL was insufficient to retain our equity percentage so we would be diluted significantly and we would have a great deal less involvement in the business than we normally like to have for the level of investment. And finally, we felt the return on our investment would not be sufficient. So in the end we took a straight commercial decision that there were better investments which could earn us more money.'

PPL is continuing to make steady progress towards producing a small herd of genetically modified sheep capable of producing AAT in their milk. In the spring of 1992 it was demonstrated that lambs could inherit the genetically modified gene. Seven such lambs were born to seven different ewes having inherited the gene from one genetically modified ram and produced milk in spring 1992 which contained very similar commercially viable quantities of AAT.

The company is close to merging with a smaller US company which would give the merged entity production facilities on both sides of the Atlantic. PPL was close to cash break-even in 1992 and hopes to 'go public' in late 1993 or early 1994.

Chapter Nine

The Club

Club 18–30's reputation for exporting lager loutishness to the beaches of Europe was probably largely unfounded but, when Harry Goodman's International Leisure Group (ILG) went bust in March 1991, it was the demise of Club 18–30 more than ILG's Intasun or Air Europe subsidiaries which attracted all the tabloid headlines.

What all those stories of cheap booze and easy sex ignored was that Club 18–30 was extremely profitable. ILG was brought down by the rapid expansion of its airline, Air Europe, which, when bookings dried up at the time of the Gulf War, found itself the owner of too many half-empty aircraft. Club 18–30 was a victim of the ILG crash, not one of its causes.

By the time the BBC started filming in September 1991, Club 18–30 had already risen phoenix-like from the ashes as The Club. Within five weeks of the collapse of ILG, The Club's managing director, Jeremy Muller, had managed to get venture capital backing to buy the brand name Club 18–30 from the administrator, obtained all the necessary permits from the Civil Aviation Authority (CAA) and the Association of British Travel Agents (ABTA), and produced a summer brochure and got it on to the travel agents' racks.

It was a remarkable achievement. Jeremy Muller and The Club's youthful management team hardly had time to draw breath. But then they knew there was not a moment to lose. If they had failed to get a brochure out for the summer season, the contacts with the old Club 18–30 hoteliers would have been severed and the company would have lost a year's trading and a great deal of good will in the resorts. Such a loss of momentum would have made the company's resurrection almost impossible.

It also illustrates that when it really matters there are some venture capitalists who can move fast and work to a deadline. Jeremy Muller explained that without County NatWest Ventures and Grosvenor the deal would never have got done:

'We had to have the finance in place within three weeks. Some of the potential suitors fell away very quickly when they realized they couldn't possibly comply with our time scale. That left us with County NatWest, Grosvenor and a third institution which was tremendously enthusiastic and supportive but which when it came to it, was very nervous about committing funds.

'It put us in a very precarious position as far as the two lead investors were concerned because they were relying on the third investor. This was literally within 24 hours of the deal being signed and if County and Grosvenor hadn't agreed to cover for the third investor and to seek another partner later, the deal wouldn't have been done.'

Janis Anderson was the Grosvenor executive responsible for its investment in The Club. It was Janis who worked all hours and all through one night to get the deal through and she is now a director of the company. The Club is an example of the kind of deal which Grosvenor is good at. When Grosvenor started fundraising for fresh investment funds in the spring of 1992, the Club was often cited as the sort of deal where Grosvenor, ever quick on its feet, is better placed than many of its competitors.

It was the beginning of February 1992. The Club had a successful first summer season and the company made an operating profit in its first year of around £300 000. The board was now meeting to consider whether it should launch a winter ski programme.

One of the strongest impressions which emerged from this book was just how well most of the entrepreneurs – even those with initial doubts – get on with their venture capital partners once the deal is done. However, here is an example of how managers and venture capitalists sometimes approach a problem from a different perspective, how the financial orientation of venture capitalists can lead to a particular view of a company's needs and how entrepreneurs like Jeremy Muller learn to understand it.

Club 18–30 had run skiing holidays since 1979 taking between 2000 and 3000 people during the early 1980s. In 1986, Club 18–30 pioneered the 'learn to ski' concept, the first fully comprehensive ski package tour which included travel, accommodation, the hire of skis, tuition and lift passes. This formula proved very successful and by the late 1980s the company was carrying around 7500 people each winter.

Jeremy Muller and his team had prepared a presentation for the board which was meeting at the City offices of County NatWest Ventures. The Club's management team had the enthusiasm of youth and while there was no doubt that Jeremy Muller was in charge, he gave the impression of being able to combine an open style of management with great professionalism. There was also an energy and high spiritedness which didn't stand on ceremony. Stuart Hayward, the overseas commercial director, opened the meeting by cracking open a bottle of Schnapps and demonstrating the correct way to hold the minute glass between the thumb and little finger and downing it in one gulp in true après ski fashion. Everyone got a glass. Schnapps is an acquired taste and Janis left hers.

Jeremy Muller had had a change of plan. His designers originally came up with the idea of using a distinctively designed fold-out sheet for the Club's first winter ski programme. At the last minute he had decided that wouldn't work. Getting a brochure on to the travel agents' racks is the key to selling holidays and Jeremy was worried that the fold-out sheet's awkward size might mean that it wouldn't get racked or would get lost among the large brochures. It had been decided to go for the more traditional brochure format, although in a style which would make it stick out from the competition. The Club's distinctive logo was usually seen over an upside down triangle in a circle. The triangle had now been reversed to form a snow topped mountain.

Jeremy Muller said almost no one else was offering skiing holidays specifically aimed at the youth market. Most of The Club's winter travellers would be first-time skiers who need the reassurance that they can make a fool of themselves in the company of other people like themselves. Interestingly, experience from the old Club 18–30 days indicated that there was very little overlap between the summer and winter holidaymakers; few Club 18–30 summer holidaymakers took winter skiing holidays and vice versa.

Jeremy Muller explained the philosophy behind The Club's skiing holidays: 'There is nothing worse than being dumped in a foreign ski school. We do everything to encourage people. We guarantee that they will learn at least how to turn and stop and that they will be taught by like-minded people in an informal atmosphere.'

The ski market is not huge. There are 800 000 regular skiers in the UK and between 375 000 and 400 000 ski each year, although as chairman Francis Higgins pointed out it gets a lot of column inches coverage in the press. The main operators are Falcon, and Enterprise, both part of Owners Abroad, Thomson, Neilson, and Crystal. Thomson had launched Skistyle aimed at younger skiers, but Jeremy Muller said the approach lacked focus.

The Club planned to sell only 4000 holidays for the winter of 1992/93, so initially at least the company was only aiming for a very small market share. The brochure would be launched towards the end of June with 24 pages and Jeremy was convinced that with The Club brand name the brochure would be prominently displayed.

According to The Club's figures, if the winter ski brochure was a sell out it would make a net contribution to profits of £30 000 covering an additional overhead of £160 000. Of course there was no guarantee that this would happen and, as Jeremy Muller admitted, it was difficult to justify in financial terms but then he had other reasons for wanting to introduce a winter programme. It was all part of his campaign to establish The Club name as a credible and comprehensive brand in the market place with a year-round presence on the travel agents' shelves. The travel agents kept asking the company if it intended returning with a ski programme and Jeremy Muller feared that The Club would not be considered well established until it was operating in both summer and winter markets. There was also the benefit of being able to offer year-round employment to the best summer staff and resort managers which reduced the risk of highly trained people being lured away by other operators.

Jeremy warned that if they didn't sell as many holidays as they expected the ski programme might lose as much as £100 000. Jeremy felt this was a risk worth taking. He described the opportunity as good public relations; it could also be described as investing in the brand.

The investors were not convinced. Janis thought Jeremy was being optimistic when he said he could sell 4000 holidays after a two-year break from the ski market. It was established that The Club would need to sell between 3000 and 3500 holidays to break even and that a loss of up to £100 000 would arise if fewer than 1000 holidays were sold.

Both Janis and Barrie Moore from County NatWest Ventures were worried that potentially the company could lose a lot of money. Barrie had thought that overhead recovery was the rationale for the winter programme with a contribution to profits if sales went well. He was concerned that they could be questioning the whole financial viability of the company by launching a ski programme at this time.

The chairman, Francis Higgins, wondered if there was any way to reduce the risk. The meeting then explored the possibility of compromise. By scaling down the launch cost and printing fewer brochures, the additional marketing overhead could be brought down to between £60 000 and £70 000 which would be sufficient to get the brochure to the key agents until there was some idea of how the bookings were going. On that basis, Jeremy calculated he could break even with around 2000 passengers.

The investors wanted to go away and think about it, but Jeremy was firm that it was not a decision which could wait until the next board meeting on 18 March. If there was to be a ski brochure he would need to have photographers in the resorts before the snow went, and that meant next week. As he said there was nothing so unconvincing as ski brochures with no snow.

Later that week Janis telephoned Jeremy Muller to reconfirm the go ahead with certain provisos. She and Barrie Moore from County NatWest Ventures wanted him to keep down the cost of the winter ski programme to the level at which it would break even carrying between 2000 and 2500 passengers. Janis described a cautious way of funding the major part of the programme in a manner which wouldn't necessarily affect the projections in the business plan. The biggest expense was marketing and Janis recalled that Jeremy had underspent his marketing budget for the summer programme. She suggested that the cost of marketing the summer programme should now be frozen and that the savings should be diverted to funding the new winter programme.

The investors and the shareholder managers had reached a compromise but it left Jeremy Muller with the feeling that the institutions didn't quite take on board the meaning of the winter programme:

'We made it very clear that it wasn't necessarily designed to make a substantial contribution to profits; it was designed as much as a flagwaving, public relations exercise, particularly in respect of the retail travel trade. They were much more concerned with the financial implications. At one point one of the institutional directors suggested that this could possibly bring the company down. In fact that is absolute nonsense. The relative size of the winter programme and the risks involved are tiny when compared to the summer programme.

'They were much more concerned with the bottom line but in the end we reached a compromise. We can now produce a brochure which, as far as the retail trade and our customers are concerned, is as large or as small as they want to think it is. It's all in the eye of the beholder.'

Jeremy Muller said he had no preconceived idea of what it would be like working with venture capitalists:

'I'm pleased to say that the experience has been excellent. I have a great deal of admiration for them. They are Jacksof-all trades and masters of none. **They certainly understand the balance sheet, and they have interesting techniques for trying to understand what lies behind the business and its potential for success.**

'You have to admire their ability to dip in and out of all sorts of industries and all sorts of sectors at a moment's notice if a deal becomes available. Sometimes they must make very quick decisions because they are in the business of investing money to live. For example, on the day The Club deal was signed, Barrie Moore and the team from County NatWest Ventures had to leave the celebrations at four o'clock on a Friday afternoon to visit a sausage skin maker.'

He believes that there is a delicate balance to be struck between entrepreneur and venture capitalist even if in the last analysis the venture capitalist has very little option but to let the entrepreneur get on with running the business.

'I'm personally very open with the investors as to our successes and our failures. But it's up to the investors to allow us to continue to run the business. Ultimately, and I say this without menace, they don't have very much of a veto.

'There are five of us in this particular company who are running the show and should the investors choose to take an opposite view and require us to change our strategy radically or change our thinking radically we could choose not to go along with them and they are left high and dry. To put it bluntly, if it doesn't suit them and we can't come to a compromise then we could walk out the door. In the case of this particular company they have nearly £2 million riding on this investment.'

Janis sees the relationship differently. She said:

'All managers think they are the only people who can actually do the job. And certainly when we invest in a company we do so because we believe the management can deliver what they have promised. Investors will continue to back the management for as long as they continue to perform. But if they start making a mess of it, it might be appropriate for us to intervene and either strengthen or change the management. There have been two companies during my time at Grosvenor where we have all but changed the entire management.'

At the beginning of December 1992, Jeremy Muller, was well satisfied with The Club's progress:

'In what was considered to be one of the worst years that the packaged travel industry has ever experienced, the number of summer travellers taking holidays with The Club rose from 18 000 in 1991 to 41 000 in 1992. This was in line with our business plan. We also outperformed our only real competitor, Twenty's Holidays, which is part of Owners Abroad, and we are now firmly placed as the preferred brand in the young person's packaged holiday market.'

Tour operators reported a 20 per cent drop in winter ski holiday bookings for the 1992/93 season. Against this background The Club was pleased with the level of bookings for the early part of its first skiing season, although in March Jeremy Muller admitted that a combination of oversupply together with dreadful snow conditions in January and February had led to a lower than expected level of bookings.

Chapter Ten

Holograms

Edward Tydda has a passionate belief in holograms. He has been working with them for 12 years, and for the last three years he has been developing a revolutionary new method of bonding them on to fabric.

Holograms have been around since 1963 and yet they have failed to make a big impact on the fashion industry. Edward was convinced that this was because no one had found a satisfactory way of getting them to stay fixed on to fabric. This was the problem which Edward had now solved.

But unlike a lot of scientists would have done, Edward had put a lot of time and effort into finding out if the fashion market was really interested in holograms. He had researched the market himself and manufacturers and retailers had told him they would use his service to put holograms on a range of clothing from baseball caps to sweatshirts.

He now needed £1.5 million to set up a factory, start production and hire a sales team. Edward had approached Grosvenor because he had been told that Grosvenor was keen on technology and had a reputation for innovation.

On the face of it Edward Tydda's operation looked a likely candidate for venture capital. His proposition involved the commercial exploitation of a high technology British invention with a market apparently ready to be exploited. It was Edward's view that if he couldn't get the funds to exploit his invention commercially, there had to be something wrong with the way Britain's financial institutions finance innovation.

Edward was reluctant to believe this, but by the time he reached Grosvenor, he had already been rejected by over 70 banks and other financial institutions. Would Grosvenor be prepared to stick its neck out and back this high risk start up?

Edward Tydda's passion for holograms began by accident as he explained:

'I worked as a motorcycle courier and one day I happened to visit a hologram company. I couldn't believe what I saw. There was a gun hanging on the wall and I thought the company made guns. It turned out to be a hologram. The chap offered me a job which was how I started doing holography. I began at the bottom, cleaning the toilets, laying the carpets and painting the walls but within three months I was actually shown how to make a hologram. I ended up as sales director and took the company's turnover up to just under £400 000 per annum.'

Up until now holograms had been attached to clothing with hot melted adhesive and only one type of hologram, the silver embossed variety, like those seen on credit cards, had been available. According to Edward Tydda this method had proved unreliable. The adhesive tended to lose its effectiveness in the wash; items which have been bonded by heat get unbonded when they are washed or ironed.

One major high street retailer which sold a sweatshirt with a hologram design thought it had a major winner on its hand until shoppers brought them back complaining that the hologram came off.

Edward Tydda and his team which included his brother, Richard, are the kind of people who forget to eat, and work through the night when they think they are on to something. However, Edward was trying hard to get away from the mad boffin image which surrounds many of the people who work with holograms. He was keen to give his company a more professional image. Companies which are driven by their technical expertise often forget that technical innovation doesn't amount to much unless they can first stop it being copied and second sell it.

This was the mistake which Edward was determined not to make. Edward had to prove that the market was there and that his invention could be protected: 'We did this by going to trade exhibitions and collecting the names and addresses of the people that said they wanted to use it. The next stage was to make sure the machine could be protected by patents and insurance.'

Edward found that the samples which they had made up were generating so much interest that he started to look round for sources of finance to start manufacturing: 'It had become clear that the market we were aiming at had hardly been exploited in any way, shape or form. With that in mind and a brief business plan I actually visited over 70 banks hoping and praying to get the venture capital we required.'

Edward had managed to interest Disney in Florida and Eurodisney in the process, but even the magic of Disney failed to impress the financiers and he drew a blank with all of them. He then decided to seek professional help. He appointed City accountants Neville Russell and together they produced a new business plan. It was this business plan which was now being considered by Grosvenor.

The plan was to exploit the technology in two areas: one was to actually make the holograms and apply them to clothing to customers' own designs; the other was to licence the machine and technology around the world.

To date the company had been run on a shoestring with the backing of friends, family and potential customers. Edward Tydda had personally invested £150 000. Many entrepreneurs, including several featured in this book, are initially at least very sceptical as to whether or not they want a venture capitalist breathing down their necks telling them how to run their business.

Edward Tydda would positively welcome it. He felt he needed more than just money:

'We want help, advice and guidance from our financiers. We are good holographers, but there are areas where we lack experience. We need a hand in hand rather than an arm round the shoulder approach from a venture capitalist. If

we can't succeed then basically this market isn't there for anybody. My team has invested a lot of time and a lot of money and their heart and souls are in this project. We owe it to them and to our industry to succeed.'

It was the beginning of February 1992 and Trevor Bayley and Stephen Edwards from Grosvenor were in a taxi on their way to Neville Russell for their first meeting with Edward Tydda.

Trevor is enthusiastic: 'I don't think I have seen anything in the last six months where intuitively I feel there is a huge potential market.' However, this was a start up with inexperienced managers in a high risk business which meant they would have a difficult job persuading their colleagues at Grosvenor that here was a company worth backing.

At Grosvenor it is the younger executives who often have the job of initially assessing the companies which approach them for finance. Some executives do have a speciality, but otherwise the work is allocated in what looks like an arbitrary fashion: it could be a matter of who took the first telephone call from an entrepreneur enquiring if Grosvenor would be interested in seeing their business plan, or it could be simply a question of whose work load looks the lightest.

At this level the big satisfaction of the job is finding a company which Grosvenor will be prepared to back and executives can find it frustrating if they get a long line of companies to investigate which don't amount to much or for which there is little support within Grosvenor.

If an executive is keen on a particular deal, he or she must persuade colleagues within Grosvenor to back his or her judgement and get the bandwagon rolling. Grosvenor executives talk about 'selling' deals and some deals are characterized as 'difficult to sell'. Edward Tydda's hologram process was one of them.

There is a view within Grosvenor that people who get involved with holograms, are either scientists or artists, whereas what venture capitalists are actually looking for are people who can exploit what they are doing commercially.

Edward Tydda had brought various samples to show Trevor and

Stephen. His method of bonding holograms on to fabric could also be used for bonding other types of plastic to fabric as well. Edward explained that they had been working on bonding luminous, reflective and fluorescent plastic images on to fabric which could be used on jackets, socks and scarves. These would be particularly useful in children's clothing to help them stay safe at night. For example, a child is much more likely to be happy to wear a jacket with a reflective picture of Michael Jackson or Batman on it than they are the traditional reflective bands which are now available.

And although this was not something which Edward had actively explored yet, the fact that his machine could also bond fabric to fabric might mean that there were some circumstances where it could replace the sewing machine.

When Trevor and Stephen first arrived at the meeting Edward had handed them both a hologram of a crown to stick on their lapel. The image was so realistic that they looked as if they had a small gold crown pinned to their jackets. This was a photopolymer hologram – what Edward described as the bees knees – an American technology which only Edward's process could bond on to fabric.

Until now all Edward's experiments had been on man-made fibres. They were currently working on cotton and the results looked promising but it took time to complete the 100 washes needed to test the durability of the bond.

Trevor and Stephen left the meeting still convinced there was a huge fashion market for holograms. They now saw that the importance of this proposal lay not so much in the holograms themselves but in the technology which bonded them to fabric. What worried Trevor and which he decided needed more investigation was why no one had done it before. Edward informed them that a major international company had spent £3 million trying to develop a technique for bonding holograms onto fabric shoes.

Trevor was not reassured by this story; he thought that if a major industrial company couldn't do it, there was perhaps the possibility that either Edward's technology didn't work or the market simply wasn't there. And, in spite of all Edward's attempts to present himself as a capable manager, Trevor's impression was that he was a 'bit of a boffin'.

Four days later, Stephen phoned John Hammond at Neville Russell, Edward's adviser, to tell him that Grosvenor were not interested in backing Edward's company. Stephen said that while Grosvenor were impressed with the product they didn't think that the management was strong enough. Stephen was convinced that Edward would find a way of getting his process into production. He suggested that Edward might have more success in raising the money he needed from a trade investor. For example, Edward might be able to find a company in the fashion or textile industry which would be prepared to back him with money and marketing advice.

But Edward was not downhearted. Later on in February he talked to Richard Branson's Virgin group who were interested in becoming investors and he had not entirely ruled out venture capital. But, like a lot of people who knock on venture capital's door only to find a brick wall, Edward was very depressed when he failed to raise the money this way. He left with the impression that venture capitalists are reluctant to take a risk. He realized that raising money for start ups is exceedingly difficult. Even so he believed that they were only interested in cast iron solid returns. He had got the feeling that unless he could produce cheques from actual customers the money wouldn't be forthcoming. As he said, if his customers were backing him with money, he wouldn't need to look for venture capital.

But Edward was out to confound all those financiers who showed him the door. He decided to put his search for venture capital on hold in order to rewrite his business plan. Still determined to start manufacturing, he found support in one of the big clearing banks. In the end it was the small business manager at his local branch of the Midland Bank in Harrow which provided some help to move into manufacturing.

At the beginning of December 1992, Edward and his team were installed in a 5500-square-foot office and factory in Alperton on London's North Circular road. This was a big advance from the 400-square-foot garage in which they had started. The orders were flowing in and the two machines were working flat out. This was in line with Edward's forecasts in the business plan, and there are plans to increase the number of machines.

The last year had taken its toll though: Edward lost two stone in weight and it's still a hand to mouth existence. Edward and his brother Richard are not drawing any wage. Edward lives at home, and he is reliant on his family and friends.

It's a high cost to pay but, as Edward says, if you believe in something 110 per cent you don't have any other option. The gamble looks as if it may be paying off. They have been producing Batman T-shirts with Warner Brothers; they are about to sign an agreement with a manufacturers' agent who produces 200 million labels a year and who wants to develop reflective labels for the fashion industry; and there is still the possibility of some sort of cooperative venture with Richard Branson amongst others.

If a venture capitalist walked in now waving a cheque, Edward says he would only do a deal on his terms.

143

Chapter Eleven

Midland Independent Newspapers

Midland Independent Newspapers is one of Britain's leading regional newspaper groups. Its flagship newspaper, the *Birmingham Evening Mail*, an evening tabloid with a circulation of over 200 000, was named UK regional newspaper of the year by the UK Press Gazette in 1992.

The group publishes around 20 titles. These include the *Birmingham Post* a regional daily broadsheet newspaper with a circulation of around 26 000 in the Midlands where its business pages are read by more managers than the *Financial Times*.

The management completed a £125 million management buyout in November 1991 lead by Candover and CINVen, two of the country's largest venture capitalists, the latter being the venture capital arm of British Coal, British Rail and Barclays Bank Pension Funds.

Candover and CINVen then decided to sell up to £12 million-worth of their investment in Midland Independent Newspapers to other venture capitalists. Grosvenor was asked if they would be interested.

This is the process known as syndication*. It is very common on big deals like this where one venture capitalist, or in this case two, does all the research needed to arrive at a decision to invest on the understanding they can then sell some of their shares on to other investors. Sometimes this process of syndication is done after the deal is completed which is what was happening at Midland Independent, when the process is often referred to as sell-down.

Grosvenor put Trevor Bayley to work on the deal. He didn't spend as much time investigating the business as he would have done if Grosvenor had been the lead investor. However, he couldn't take it as read that the endorsement of such heavyweights as Candover and CINVen meant that Midland Independent Newspapers Limited was a sound business, and he only had a relatively short time to get a good grasp of the business.

Venture capitalists who are following rather than leading a deal must satisfy themselves that the deal leader has done its due diligence properly; that it has got all the legal details right, and that it has then reached the right conclusion about the business and has got the right management in place. Once they are satisfied that all these aspects have been correctly assessed, and once they have completed their own researches, a deal follower will then make the final decision on price.

It is not unknown for a deal follower to alter the terms of a deal, but it is rare. In most cases, the price is set by the deal leader, and the deal follower must either take it or leave it. Grosvenor's Robert Drummond characterizes the true venture capital deal as one where the company and the venture capitalist work in partnership to develop the business. At Midland Independent Newspapers, if Grosvenor decided to become an investor, it was unlikely to play an active role in the management of the company. Having decided that Midland Independent Newspapers was a good business, the decision to invest would be determined on price. What Trevor had to decide was whether Grosvenor thought that Candover and CINVen had paid a full price for Midland Independent Newspapers or whether they bought it cheaply.

There is something about newspapers which attracts entrepreneurs and investors alike. It was an attraction which proved fatal for Robert Maxwell and financially damaging for others such as Eddie Shah who, in breaking the stranglehold of the print unions, enabled the rest of the industry to introduce new computer technology. It has also attracted some of the most controversial entrepreneurs of their generation. Men like Rupert Murdoch and Conrad Black who in turning round inefficiently-run newspapers have gone on to exploit their positive cash flow to build multi-million-pound, multinational-media empires.

Wednesday, 27 November 1991

Trevor went to Birmingham to meet the management team at Midland Independent Newspapers. Jonathan Clarke of CINVen and another potential investor, Paolo Sassetti, were also there. Trevor explained the background to the buy-out:

'Midland Independent Newspapers, or the Birmingham Post and Mail Limited as it was then called, was bought by a wealthy American, Ralph Ingersoll, in 1988. He ran it from a distance and according to the current management he tried to impose certain operating styles on the business which weren't appropriate for a provincial newspaper in this country.

'The American company has had financial problems in the US and now in the UK, so it put the business up for sale in the summer of this year [1991] and the management were obviously very keen to buy the business. The current management team has only been together for two or three years. They put an offer together with the help of Candover and CINVen, and they completed the buy-out a couple of weeks ago.

'The purpose of the meeting today is to have a trip round the main facility in the centre of Birmingham and then to have a presentation from the management. The total deal was £125 million of which £60 million was provided by the two venture capital houses. The rest of the funding came in the form of £50 million-worth of bank finance and £15 million-worth of mezzanine finance* which is an intermediate layer of capital between share capital and bank debt.'

Trevor's first reaction was that Candover and CINVen paid a full price. The *Evening Mail* is very dependent on recruitment advertising. A page of recruitment advertising is the highest yielding category of advertising. Newspapers carry heavy fixed costs so profits are very sensitive to any change in advertising revenue.

Most people take their newspapers for granted, never giving the process by which they are produced a second thought. It's easy to forget that newspapers are produced in factories by workers; they are not just the work of journalists sitting behind computer terminals. Unlike London where, with the move out of Fleet Street, the editorial and printing functions are now largely performed on separate sites, the Birmingham Post newspapers are still produced and printed from the same address in the centre of Birmingham.

It was the day following the death of Queen lead singer, Freddie Mercury. 'Freddie dies of Aids,' screamed the headline on the first edition of the *Evening Mail*. Trevor was meeting John Whitehouse, the group finance director. The offices are a rabbit warren of soulless corridors. Visitors are not allowed to find their own way round for fear that some Kafkaesque fate might befall them. So John Whitehouse sent his secretary down to escort Trevor.

As they waited for Jonathan Clarke and Paolo Sassetti, John Whitehouse took Trevor through the group's titles. There are two rarities: a Saturday sports paper, the *Sports Argus* and a regional Sunday, the *Sunday Mercury*, which has a circulation of 150 000 and outsells all other Sunday newspapers in Birmingham. The group also publishes the *Coventry Evening Telegraph* in Coventry with a circulation of 87 000.

There is also a weekly division which produces freesheets: four in Birmingham and two in Coventry. The group had contemplated selling the freesheets but now intended retaining them. And there are several contracts to print newspapers for other companies, most notably for Thomson Regional Newspapers.

Trevor owned up to a childhood spent partly in Birmingham, a period of his life which ignited a lifetime's loyalty to the 'Blues', as Birmingham City Football Club are known.

With the arrival of Jonathan Clarke and Paolo Sassetti the group started their long trek round Midland Independent's various departments. No one would have been surprised if John Whitehouse's secretary had produced several packets of Kendal Mint Cake.

Passing down a corridor which overlooks the editorial floor John Whitehouse pointed out that although the *Post* and *Evening Mail* were both produced there, they maintained separate editorial teams. And altogether the group employed 230 journalists there and in the branches. They were linked up to the other offices and to the wire services by computer. However, the newspapers weren't fully electronic yet. The pages could be partly laid out on the computer, but the next development was to go over to full page make up.

'Welcome to the best classified department in the Midlands' is the message which greeted the party as they entered the tele ad department where 80 saleswomen sat on the telephone taking down the ads and skillfully persuading people that by spending just a little bit more on their ad, by adding extra words or putting the ad in a box – there are any number of tricks of the trade – their ad was much more likely to succeed.

This was the department which held the key to the group's prosperity. Selling classified advertisements was the *Evening Mail*'s most important revenue-gathering activity. The paper normally had a ratio of 40 to 45 per cent of advertising to editorial, so for every six pages of editorial there would be at least four pages of advertising.

'It's the magic of Christmas' was scrawled across the wall in red and surrounded by flashing neon. More in exhortation than in greetings, it was evidence that the department was in the middle of its Christmas sales campaign.

Somewhere further along the endless labyrinth of corridors, a door opened and the visitors were ushered in to meet Ian Dowell, the *Evening Mail*'s editor. Thursday, the main day for job ads, is the biggest selling day. When job advertising peaked in 1989 and 1990 there were as many as 64 pages of job ads in the paper. They had now fallen to around 15 which was apparently a lot better than the competition. They could sell as many as 30 000 extra copies on a Thursday.

Ian Dowell was working on ideas which would bring in a niche readership on other days of the week. For example a jobs supplement was planned for Mondays, which would carry editorial features on the jobs market. On Tuesday there were ideas for an eight-page colour supplement for women. On Wednesday there might be a mid-week sports special covering all the sports which didn't get covered over the weekend, such as darts and the local school and junior soccer leagues, where the paper reckoned there was a massive untapped market.

On Saturday the *Argus* managed to sell 46 000 copies. The point of a Saturday sports paper is to get the football results to people. It is only possible to do this by about ten to six in the evening just when the traditional newsagents are closing. The *Argus* had got round this problem by developing a good relationship with the 'open all hours' corner shops.

With the exception of John Whitehouse, the rest of the management team had spent the morning meeting the management in the Coventry office. The management team had now returned to Birmingham to meet their potential new investors. Chris Oakley, the managing director, had an editorial background in regional newspapers having been deputy editor of the *Yorkshire Post*, editor of the *Lancashire Evening Post* and editor of the *Liverpool Echo*. He joined the Birmingham Post and Mail two years ago as editor-in-chief and deputy managing director, becoming managing director in April of last year.

As he said, the last ten days since they signed the management buy-out deal had been spent catching up on some of the day-to-day management tasks which got neglected during the six months which it had taken to do the buy-out.

Chris Oakley introduced the rest of the team: Ernest Petrie, the managing director of the Coventry operation was an accountant with long experience of regional newspapers mainly with Thomsons; John Whitehouse they had already met; Julian Day, the commercial director, he described as the most innovative in regional newspapers, building sales and revenues where others were failing; Terry Page, the editor-in-chief; and Joe Holmes, the operations director who was dubbed indefatigible.

Their business plan set out how the group intended reducing costs and increasing advertising revenue. On the costs side of the equation, the group intended shedding 120 jobs, a programme which had already been started and which would mean savings of £1.5 million by 1993/94. On the revenue side, it was planned to reduce the reliance on job ads and the company was making a big effort to persuade the national advertisers of the benefits of advertising regionally.

Trevor wanted to know if the levels of advertising achieved in 1989/90 were the best the company had ever achieved. According to Julian Day there were similar peaks in 1973/74 and 1979/80 and that they were getting the earliest indication of a pick up just now in the business cycle with an upturn forecast for the second quarter of 1992. There was also substantial inward investment in Birmingham with new jobs being created by TSB, Toyota and British Gas.

150 Monday, 9 December 1991

CINVen wanted to complete the syndication by Christmas and Jonathan Clarke was asking Trevor for a decision. Trevor needed to decide today whether or not to commit Grosvenor to the deal in principle. The minimum which Grosvenor could put in was £1 million which meant that this was going to be a deal which would need to go to the investment committee before it got the final go ahead.

Trevor had decided to talk the deal over with Robert before giving CINVen any undertaking. Robert knows about the newspaper industry. He is a director of South News plc, a weekly newspaper group in and around London. Trevor started from the position that Midland Independent was a good business but the price fully valued the company. However, if Robert thought the price was acceptable, he would be happy to see the deal go through. Robert may know his newspapers but he had never been seduced by the romance of the business.

As it turned out Robert shared Trevor's view. Robert was doubtful if the group would see any upturn in recruitment advertising in 1992. South News had seen sitsvac advertising, as it is called in the trade, decline by 50 per cent in each of the last two years. It was his view that the situation in Birmingham might lag behind the South East and that they could see a further fall in 1992.

He was also worried that over the long term, the group's longstanding classified advertising monopoly in Birmingham might be eroded by the arrival of operations like *Loot*, a weekly magazine which offered free small ads to individuals but which sold for a high cover price.

The current volatility of newspaper profits made Robert uneasy about valuing the business solely on the basis of its earnings. Looking at sales instead, he worked out that the group had been bought for about twice its annual turnover which he reckoned was about the price newspapers were changing hands for at the height of the merger mania of the last years of the 1980s.

Robert felt that Candover and CINVen had paid a full price for the group. Robert didn't tell Trevor what to think; that is not Robert's management style. He was still talking about Trevor preparing a paper for the investment committee. However, Robert found it exceedingly difficult not to act decisively.

He thought the decision should come from Trevor. Instead of instructing him to drop the deal, he put the ball back in Trevor's court by telling him he wouldn't be unhappy if Trevor said he didn't want to go any further with the deal. Trevor got the message; there was part of him which didn't like closing the door on a good business but in the end he was happy to defer to Robert's view that the deal looked fully priced, especially as this was the conclusion which he had already reached himself. Grosvenor decided not to back Midland Independent.

At the end of October 1992, Midland Independent Newspapers published its results for the six months to the end of June. This was the first financial statement since the management buy-out. It shows a fourfold increase in operating profits to £7.3 million. With a similar second half performance, profits for the year should come out at around £14.6 million. Managing director Chris Oakley professed himself well satisfied with the result given the economic climate.

As it turned out Robert Drummond was right to predict a further decline in recruitment advertising. However, Chris Oakley says Grosvenor failed to appreciate Midland Independent's ability to cut costs and reduce its reliance on job ads. The group managed to increase its share of the regional advertising market and continued to persuade national brand advertisers of the merits of regional advertising.

Still, Robert Drummond didn't regret Grosvenor's decision not to invest in Midland Independent although he acknowledged that when job advertising picked up, there would be an almost immediate and dramatic improvement in profits.

Jonathan Clarke of CINVen said: 'We are happy that Midland's results bear out our judgement that this was a sound investment.'

Chapter Twelve

Fundraising

By the end of 1991 Grosvenor was beginning to think about raising more money to invest. Two of Grosvenor's funds were all but fully invested, and a third would be fully invested by the end of 1992. Grosvenor's first fund, Grosvenor Development Capital, a quoted investment trust, reinvests the money it gets when an investment is sold, but the amounts available from this source wouldn't be sufficient to maintain Grosvenor's projected level of investment. The other three funds return the money to investors when an investment is sold.

Robert Drummond had to go out and sell Grosvenor and the idea of venture capital to investors, such as pension funds and insurance companies, who were very nervous about the economic climate in general and venture capital in particular.

Many banks, insurance companies and pension funds make their own investments in venture capital and get their funds from a benevolent parent. Independent firms like Grosvenor must find their own investors and in the middle of a recession which has hit small businesses particularly hard, finding investors whose portfolios weren't bearing the scars of over-optimistic forays into venture capital during the late 1980s was clearly not going to be easy.

This was the moment when Robert Drummond and his team at Grosvenor got a taste of their own medicine. Here was a group of people which spent its working life judging the relative merits of the numerous entrepreneurs who approach them for money. Now the boot was on the other foot and it was Grosvenor's turn to experience what all those entrepreneurs have to go through: the months of uncertainty, the constant need to explain and justify, the endless hours spent on the phone, the time spent in gruelling meetings, the never ending demand for additional facts and figures.

Tony Crook, Michael Glover and Bill Edge had all experienced the agonies of fundraising before, although of the three, Tony Crook was the one most closely involved with Grosvenor's previous fundraising efforts.

Robert Drummond helped raise an investment fund during his time at Electra and he was peripherally involved in fundraising at Alta Berkeley where he worked for a brief period during the early 1980s. But this was the first time that he had raised a new fund at Grosvenor and as Grosvenor Venture Managers' single biggest shareholder – he has 40 per cent of the shares – he was also the person with most at stake.

Before joining Grosvenor, Robert worked mainly in organizations financed by the big clearing banks, where he was not required to set out his stall and attract investors. But Robert was not daunted by the challenge.

'I have always considered myself a salesman. I'm a salesman when I'm talking to people I wish to invest in. On the face of it they have got to sell to me because I've got the money and they want it. Actually it's not quite like that. If I like their business and I want to invest in it because I think I have spotted a big winner, the odds are they are quite capable of raising that money from one of my competitors.

'There is another reason why I like to sell. I like the entrepreneur to fully understand what I want, so that once we do a deal together we have a relationship that lasts and prospers. I have always been a salesman, so going out to sell my fund management capabilities is part of the same thing.'

Up until his death, Grosvenor was David Beattie. There is no doubt that within Grosvenor Robert has managed to stamp his own authority and style on the organization. Robert is a leading figure in the venture capital industry, but he is less well known among pension fund and insurance company investment managers. His chairmanship of the British Venture Capital Association (BVCA) which began in June 1992 should help raise his profile even further within the industry itself, but whether this more public role will make him better known among investors remains to be seen. The last time Grosvenor went out fundraising David Beattie was still at the helm and Robert did not underestimate just how strongly investors identified Grosvenor with David Beattie and how much they attributed the success of many of Grosvenor's early investments to his expertise.

The problem for Robert Drummond was that he couldn't point to his investment record at Grosvenor because he hadn't been there long enough. What he could do, however, was demonstrate Grosvenor's skill at realizing investments which in Robert's two years at the helm had produced an annual total of £6 million.

Grosvenor knew that if it was to meet its projected level of activity, it would need to raise a new fund sometime towards the end of 1992. For the venture capitalist, fundraising is an extremely time consuming activity. At Grosvenor this long-drawn out process began in November 1991 and it was to be well over a year before anyone knew how successful their efforts had been.

To compensate for the higher risk, investors need to be convinced that they can earn a higher return from venture capital than they can from their more mainstream investments. The problem for Grosvenor was that while its two early funds had performed well, the third and fourth funds which were raised at the top of the market in 1988 and 1989, were, in common with almost all venture capital funds raised at that time, not yet showing a positive return to their investors.

Grosvenor now had to persuade investors that it was still early days for the third and fourth funds and that once their investments began to mature they would start showing better returns. Even sophisticated investors tend to batten down the hatches and steer a safe and cautious course through a recession. Grosvenor hoped that enough investors would take the counter-cyclical view and be prepared to play the business cycles investing when everything is doom and gloom and prices are cheap and selling when everything looks hunky dory and prices are booming.

Thursday, 7 November 1991

Robert Drummond raised the question of fundraising at the weekly work-in-progress meeting. There were certain management issues to be sorted out. John Oakley, the industrialist and company doctor who chairs Grosvenor's existing funds, was 71. John Oakley had intended to retire the year before, but had stayed on after David Beattie's death. He now told Grosvenor that he definitely wanted to go. Robert said the search for a new chairman was now on and that headhunters, Tyzacks, had been asked to help.

Tony Crook had been talking to Grosvenor's existing investors about the possibility of raising a new fund. He reported a positive reaction; apparently Grosvenor's existing investors were making encouraging noises about Grosvenor's ability to raise new money.

Monday, 17 December 1991

Robert Drummond and Tony Crook met to discuss fundraising. The idea of raising the new fund through an investment trust had been rejected following discussions with the City's two best known investment trust experts, County NatWest WoodMac and Warburgs. Both had advised against going down the investment trust route. There was currently an over supply of venture capital investment trusts whose shares could be bought at big discounts to net assets. In those circumstances investors would be reluctant to put money into a new trust only to see the shares fall to an immediate discount.

Grosvenor had now more or less decided to go for the limited partnership format. This was the structure which Grosvenor used for its second, third and fourth funds where each investor becomes a limited liability partner in the fund in proportion to their investment. The limited partnership itself doesn't pay tax; instead each partner is responsible for settling their own tax bill according to their own tax status.

This format allows different types of investors to participate in the same fund. For example, pension funds and insurance companies are taxed differently but they can both become investors in the same limited partnership. The investment manager, in this case Grosvenor Venture Managers, becomes a partner too. They are generally known as the General Partner and for a small financial commitment they get a proportionately higher share in the profits once the overall return from the fund reaches a predetermined level.

The two key questions which now had to be resolved were how much should they try and raise and did they need a sponsor, such as a merchant bank, to help them.

Tony Crook reported that the existing investors were keen to keep costs down and wanted Grosvenor to go ahead without a sponsor. Robert thought they might need the added clout of a sponsor if they were to attract new investors.

This was the meeting at which Robert and Tony agreed that Grosvenor should aim to raise £60 million. It was an extremely ambitious target; if successful Grosvenor would, in one fell swoop, nearly double its funds under management; it was also over twice as much as Grosvenor raised with its third fund in the boom conditions which prevailed in 1988. However, at the end of 1991, that figure didn't look unrealistic. Grosvenor had had an encouragingly enthusiastic response from the informal soundings it had taken among its existing investors.

In addition if Grosvenor wanted to attract new investors in the United States, it would need to offer tranches of at least $10 million and as US investors are unhappy about holding more than 10 per cent of any one fund, this implied a fund size of at least $100 million or around £60 million.

At this stage no one was expecting the recession to continue into a third year and for the country to experience such a devastating collapse in consumer and business confidence with talk of the double dip bringing the worst recession since the savage deflation of the 1930s.

In the early months of 1992, the country was in the grip of election fever and Grosvenor was in no position to harden up its fundraising plans. In the middle of March, just three weeks before the general election, Grosvenor celebrated its tenth anniversary with two parties for investors and entrepreneurs at the Ironmongers' Hall, one of the City livery clubs, near the Barbican. The champagne flowed to the sound of a harp, and Robert was obviously feeling confident enough to announce that Grosvenor intended launching a new fund with a target size of £60 million.

Monday, 18 May 1992

Earlier in the month Robert had reorganized Grosvenor's management to give himself more time to devote to strategic planning and his duties as chairman of the British Venture Capital Association. He had now split the two functions of chairman and managing director. He remained as chairman but the job of managing director now fell to Michael Glover. Tony Crook, who was co-ordinating fundraising with Robert, remained a director of Grosvenor Venture Managers but was winding down his day-to-day commitments by working just three days a week. This left a hole in the fundraising team which Janis was asked to fill.

It was now Janis's job to prepare all the selling documents. These would include the letter to key investors who might be prepared to commit themselves ahead of the formal documents going out; a presentation pack outlining Grosvenor's past performance and future strategy which would be the key selling document; and finally the formal offer document.

Today, Janis, Robert and Michael Glover were meeting to discuss the letter which was to go to Grosvenor's five key investors and to set a timetable for the fundraising: when it should start, at what stage the United States should be tackled and when the offer should close.

Tuesday, 26 May 1992

It was final: the new fund was to be called the Fifth Grosvenor Fund – FGF for short. Janis proposed to close the offer on 30 November by which time they should have had in more than half of what they could expect to raise. There would be the option to extend the offer for a further 60 days to catch any stragglers, and any US investors who would only be approached in September when Grosvenor were making a series of presentations.

There was considerable disagreement on how and when the offer should be closed. Robert and Tony favoured two separate closing dates, the first earlier than the end of November, so that those investors who had made up their mind to invest, didn't have their ardour cooled by a long wait, and those that were wavering were given plenty of time to make up their minds. Michael and Janis felt this approach would encourage investors to delay making the decision to invest and that with an option to extend for 60 days or more they could in effect decide to have two closing dates.

There was also the related issue of when the formal offer document should go out. The main selling document was the information pack, and there was some disagreement as to whether investors needed to have the offer document sooner or later. In the end a consensus was reached; the offer would close at the end of October and the formal offer document wouldn't go out until September.

Thursday, 11 June 1992

Grosvenor had now found a new chairman for the funds. David Bucks, a chartered accountant who had recently retired as deputy chairman of Hill Samuel Bank, had been recruited in March. Grosvenor was now ready to embark on the first round of presentations to potential investors. Janis, with help from Stephen Edwards, Grosvenor's newest executive, who had produced most of the performance graphs and tables, had completed the presentation pack which would form the basis of Grosvenor's sales pitch to the institutions.

Robert was keen to have a mock run through ahead of tomorrow's first presentation to Scottish Investment Trust. He wanted to make sure that everyone was putting over the same message:

'We are good at dealing with the people in the businesses in which we invest and that means two things: one, we can sort out problem investments, unlike some of our competitors, and the second is that we are able to go into situations such as turnarounds and buy-ins where management changes are critical to success. Our ability to handle people comes from the experience of some of our directors in industry and our experience in venture capital.

'We are also clever. We look at cycles and we look at situations and we make investments at the right time. We are not driven by the pressures of a merchant bank, we are not driven by the pressures of a parent. If it's not good to invest in a particular year because the economy isn't right, we don't. Also we are able to do certain types of deals which other people won't tackle.

'We have the right experience and we are nimble as well as clever. We can do things in a hurry, such as the management buy-out of Elmbridge, because we can get our mind round the problem of house prices and the average life of people who are 70 years old reasonably quickly and we can negotiate in tricky situations."

Venture capital is all about having enough really good performers to pay for all the less successful investments. There is a danger that investors who can't be bothered to take a close, analytical look at Grosvenor's record will attribute the excellent performance of its first fund, Grosvenor Development Capital, to the phenomenal success of the Sage Group, the computer software company, and will dismiss it as no more than a lucky fluke. Janis was particularly concerned that they must guard against the danger of giving the impression that Sage was the only good performer in the portfolio.

It had taken Robert the good part of a year to get Grosvenor's new database up and running. It had given Stephen Edwards the raw material to be able to produce all sorts of very professional looking graphs and charts covering almost every aspect of Grosvenor's performance. Tony Crook was concerned that so much effort had gone into producing these figures that the real human stories of the many successful companies they had backed, how they came to back them, and how they responded to the Grosvenor treatment, wouldn't get through. He felt that all the facts and figures in the presentation should be brought alive with good strong case histories.

Monday, 15 June 1992

Robert and Janis were out carpet bagging. Today they were in the West End of London to see Carol Kennedy, the managing director of Pantheon Ventures. It would be a tough assignment for Robert and Janis. Carol Kennedy worked for a number of major UK pension funds and insurance companies as a specialist adviser on the selection of international venture capital funds.

Carol Kennedy has a good record. Pantheon International, the investment trust which the company she works for manages, could point to one of the best performance records in the sector returning £2017 for every £1000 invested in the five years to the end of 1992.

The poster of Magritte's surreal painting of a street scene raining bowler hatted businessmen might have been designed to catch the likes of Robert and Janis off balance. However, Robert and Janis knew Carol well. She has seen the industry from both sides: before becoming an investor she worked at Prudential Venture Managers as a venture capitalist, and her company was an investor in one of Grosvenor's funds.

Robert wanted to give Carol a formal presentation but among people who know each other well this is not always the best approach. In these circumstances Carol's style is more conversational, and is designed to extract the information she wants and needs as quickly and economically as possible.

Robert's main argument was that Grosvenor's current emphasis on management buy-ins and turnarounds was very similar to that of the early 1980s, another recessionary period, and one when Grosvenor made some of its most successful investments.

It was obviously essential that Carol understood what Grosvenor's aims and objectives were. But she also wanted hard facts about some of the recent deals, how they were structured and how they were performing; information which Robert didn't have to hand but which he agreed to send her. She was also looking for something less tangible. She said her French venture capital colleagues called it 'nose'. She described what she does as looking for patterns. For her the very best venture capitalists manage to combine intuition with sound analysis.

She is reluctant to invest before she knows how a management team works. She wants to know who is assessing the companies, who makes the final decision to back a particular enterprise, and how the after-care works. It's her view that the dynamics of the management team and how they work together is an important pointer to success. She admits she is much more likely to back funds where she knows the team and the individuals within the team and has been able to track their performance over a number of years.

Robert might not feel like the new man at Grosvenor any more, but from where Carol was sitting it was important for her to know how Robert and Janis and the team at Grosvenor were all working together and whether they could take advantage of opportunities as the market developed. Without giving a definitive no, she warned Robert and Janis that she was unlikely to back them at the moment. She put this down to the very difficult fundraising climate. US investors were not increasing their European exposure and in the UK where investors poured a lot of money into venture capital during the late 1980s, they wanted to hold back for the moment.

She said they might have more luck in early 1993. This was not much help to Robert and Janis who were hoping to have most of their new investors in place by the end of October.

Robert was getting his first hint of the difficulties which lay ahead.

Thursday, 16 July 1992

Grosvenor was already having to lower its sights. Back in December Robert and Tony agreed a fundraising target of £60 million. This was on the basis that anything less was unlikely to attract US investors. But as the initial euphoria which followed the Conservative general election victory evaporated to be replaced by ever deepening economic gloom, Grosvenor found that fundraising in its own backyard was hard going.

Grosvenor now abandoned any thoughts of a major fundraising effort in the US. To make any impact in the States in the current market they needed either to hire an intermediary or put two Grosvenor executives over there full time for around six months, neither of which they were prepared to do. It had been agreed that Robert and Janis would go to the States in September to do presentations to Grosvenor's existing US investors and anyone else who expressed an interest over the next couple of months and that would be the extent of their effort.

The draft offer document was now almost ready and Janis called in Tony Lyons, Grosvenor's public relations consultant, to finalize the press release to announce the fundraising. Most of Grosvenor's core investors still seemed keen to back the new fund, although Janis, who was talking on the telephone to four or five existing and potential investors each day, was beginning to realize just how difficult a task Grosvenor had set itself: already one major existing investor and several of the county council superannuation funds had excused themselves on the grounds that they weren't backing venture capital at the moment.

Janis's gut feeling was that they had had strong expressions of interest from investors who would invest a total of between £15 and £20 million and if the final figure came in at between £30 and £40 million it would have been a good effort. To be on the safe side and to avoid having to admit later that they had fallen short of their target, Janis agreed that for the purposes of the press release they should say they were aiming to raise £25 million.

Janis had been working almost exclusively on fundraising for the last two months and she was finding it much more time consuming than she had expected. It had obviously been a salutary experience, as she said: 'It puts us on the other side of the fence which must be good for the soul. But I have to say I prefer doing venture capital deals.'

Friday, 31 July 1992
The relentless round of presentations continued. Robert and Janis had already seen 13 existing and potential investors. Janis was on holiday, so today Robert and Tony Crook were making a pitch for the Cadbury Schweppes pension fund who were investors in Grosvenor Technology (the second fund). With the exception of one or two edgy moments including one where UK pensions manager, Hugh Edwards, rapped Robert over the knuckles for implying they only took a short-term view of their investments,

the presentation went relatively well for Grosvenor. Robert was allowed to get his message over without being sidetracked and he managed to pack in a lot of detailed information about the actual deals.

By now Robert had become used to finding the ghost of David Beattie at the feast. David Beattie once worked at Cadbury Schweppes and knew Hugh Edwards well. So it came as no surprise to Robert when Hugh Edwards admitted that David Beattie's death had given them some worries. Cadburys weren't ready to commit themselves to anything today. Nor were they prepared to make reassuring noises. Rather to Robert's surprise Hugh Edwards said he had been disappointed in the performance of the second fund. In addition Cadbury didn't put aside a specific proportion of its fund for venture capital, so Grosvenor was to be judged against all other forms of investment not just those in venture capital.

By the middle of August, Janis was back from her holiday. Since the beginning of the year, the climate for venture capital fundraising had turned very sour. This was now the most difficult period for venture capital fundraising which this generation of venture capitalists had ever experienced. The optimism which Grosvenor still felt in the spring had been replaced with a dogged determination to see this round of fundraising through. The decision was taken to put off the first closing for the new fund by a month to the end of November.

Wednesday, 23 September 1992

Robert and Janis were in the United States to talk to potential investors. They could hardly have chosen a worse time to try and persuade US investors to put money in to the UK. The United States was in the middle of an election which was likely to bring a new president to the White House and during the last week Britain had withdrawn from the ERM leaving the country's stated anti-inflation policy in tatters and the economy still showing no sign of recovery.

It was a tight schedule; they had appointments in Boston, Chicago and New York. Today, they were at the Avenue of America's headquarters of investment managers, Abbott Capital Management who have $1 billion-worth of US pension fund money under management.

The Robert and Janis show had been on the road now for four months, and there was no doubt that Robert's presentation had become very slick. He had also learnt that the world outside saw him as the new boy and that he needed to sell not only Grosvenor's track record but his own as well. He now included details of his own successes at County NatWest alongside those of Grosvenor when he was talking to potential investors. He even went to the lengths of producing a list which included not only the investments he made but also those he turned down in order to demonstrate that, although he was offered the opportunity to invest in many of the highly leveraged buy-outs of the late 1980s, he actively refused to invest in them.

Investors don't attend these presentations with their pens poised above open cheque books. Even so it was frustrating for Robert and Janis when they got no feedback at all. Obviously they couldn't expect an instant decision but some sort of indication as to whether or not the investor was even considering venture capital at that moment would have been a help.

Robert explained to Abbott chief, Ray Held, the problems they had experienced fundraising in the UK:

'It's tough, particularly because so many of the big institutions which should be investing in venture capital don't see venture capital as a distinct asset class as you do in the US. Some have also dabbled directly themselves, usually in large leveraged buy-outs which have lost them money. Then I come along and say why don't you invest in a venture capital fund and not surprisingly we find they are having difficulty differentiating what they did then from what we do now. It's a problem for the whole industry, it's not just for Grosvenor.'

In fact only two UK investors had said that they might be prepared to be named in the formal offer document as having made a commitment to invest. This was a lot less than the four or five which Grosvenor had initially hoped to attract and even now

Robert and Janis were unhappy about revealing who they were. Robert wanted to encourage investors in by the first closing date at the end of November. He let Ray Held know that they were hoping to get £20 million in by the first closing date, but that if they got significantly more they might decide to close the fund then.

Americans are renowned for their directness, but Ray Held was taken off guard when Janis bluntly asked him what his plans were. Unfortunately, the view from Abbott was not encouraging and Ray Held was forced to admit that they were not doing much overseas investment. As for Europe, he was enigmatically 'waiting for the dust to settle', without saying which particular dust: ERM dust; Maastricht dust; or Eastern European civil war dust.

As the autumn unfolded, Grosvenor realized that it hadn't been able to persuade sufficient people into its new fund to be able to get a formal offer document out in time to close the offer at the end of November as originally planned.

Grosvenor decided to extend its fundraising timetable into 1993. Janis said:

'Four investors have said they will definitely invest and are prepared to allow their names to be included in the formal offer document. I have been having long and complicated discussions with them as to what they would like to see in the formal offer document which we hope to send out early in 1993.'

Janis found the job of selling in such a hostile environment exhausting. She was also critical of the venture capital industry's seeming reluctance to produce performance statistics.

'I think Grosvenor's performance looks quite good, but I don't know how it compares to my competitors. When you are selling yourself it is a big disadvantage not being able to compare your funds with others doing a similar job.

'These figures are available in the United States. They are even available in some European countries where the venture capital industry is less well developed than here. I

wish the UK industry would do the same. There have been discussions about producing such statistics but there seems to be some reluctance to move fast. I think the industry will continue to have difficulties in fundraising until it starts producing performance figures worked out on an agreed basis.'

As chairman of the British Venture Capital Association, Robert Drummond is actively developing systems which will allow the industry to produce performance figures.

In December 1992 Robert and Janis met early one morning in his office to discuss Grosvenor's alternatives, given the disappointing level of funds committed for a first closing of the fifth fund.

They identified two options; they could delay the fund raising until March 1993 when the results of the existing Grosvenor funds for the year to December 1992 would be available. These results were expected to be very good compared to the recently published annual results of some other venture capital funds. Alternatively, they could push hard to close the fund at a low level with the existing committed investors, relying on the warmer feelings in the City towards small company prospects that Robert and Janis were optimistically beginning to hear.

They discussed the longer term structural change in the industry that appeared to be pushing the smaller independent venture capital companies towards merging, or in other ways significantly increasing their size. This would increase their 'buying power' when talking to larger pension fund and insurance company investors. They questioned whether Grosvenor might ultimately need to do this, but decided that Grosvenor's independence remains its greatest asset and any merger might compromise it. They decided therefore to push ahead hard after Christmas to have a small first closing with the investors who were close to them and understood their business. Other investors might follow once the long awaited green shoots promised by the Government appeared.

In the New Year Janis started work again, talking to investors, discussing revised terms at length with Grosvenor's solicitors and the core investors. At the same time the whole team continued to juggle the demands of its existing investments while ensuring that the life blood of Grosvenor – the making of new investments – was continued and managed effectively.

By the end of February 1993, draft agreements were ready to be circulated to investors and Grosvenor was confident a first closing of the fund would be achieved at between £6 and £10 million. This was a far cry from the original plan for a much larger new fund, but, as another venture capital company managing director had said, that can be considered quite an extraordinary achievement in the current environment.

Glossary

British Venture CapitaL Association (BVCA)

Britain's venture capital trade association covers the majority of organizations offering venture capital in this country with 115 full members at the beginning of 1992. It informs potential investors about venture capital, lobbies government, undertakes education and training, develops and maintains standards and provides a forum for the exchange of views within the industry.

Business Expansion Scheme (BES)

The scheme under which the government gives tax relief to individuals who are prepared to act as venture capitalists. Investors can back individual companies or put their money into BES funds. The original purpose of the scheme to channel private money into emerging companies was only modestly successful. In the end the popularity of BES assured tenancy schemes, which invest in residential property, and the fact that they were able to offer higher rate taxpayers almost guaranteed high returns, ensured the scheme's demise. The scheme will cease after the end of 1993.

Business Plan

This is the first document which venture capitalists generally ask to see once they have decided to investigate a company. It is likely to include the history of the company and its executives, an assessment of its products and services and the market in which they operate, its current financial position, and its plans for the future with projections of future profits and cash flow.

Business Start Up Scheme (BSS)

The government sponsored scheme which preceded the Business Expansion Scheme (BES). This scheme was intended to provide a flow of finance and expertise from nascent to established entrepreneurs in exchange for which established entrepreneurs could claim tax relief on their investment. The scheme ran for two tax years, 1981/82 and 1982/83 but failed to attract much support and was replaced by the Business Expansion Scheme in 1983.

Buy Back

The process by which a company buys its own shares. This has only been possible since 1981. For many companies which don't want to go public this may be the preferred method of providing venture capitalists with their exit proceeds.

Buy-In   see *Management Buy-In.*

Buy-Out   see *Management Buy-Out.*

Captives

The name for venture capital operations which are owned by larger financial institutions such as banks, pension funds, merchant banks or life insurance companies. Most captives rely on their owners for a flow of investment funds, although some captives also raise money from other sources as well.

Closed End

A fund with a fixed share capital, which once it is fully invested can only make further investments when it sells an investment at a profit, or raises extra money from its shareholders with a rights issue. Investment trusts are closed end funds. Closed end funds can have a fixed life, at the end of which they are wound up, or they can continue indefinitely.

Company Doctor

When a company gets into financial difficulties, its investors or bankers may demand the appointment of a new chairman or chief executive who has experience of returning ailing companies to good health, hence the expression, company doctor.

Debt Replacement Finance
Where an entrepreneur issues shares to a venture capitalist for the purpose of repaying borrowings in order to improve the company's cash flow.

Due Diligence
The investigation process which the entrepreneur must submit to before the venture capitalist finally agrees to finance the company.

Early Development Finance
The last stage of early stage finance and one which venture capitalists hope they won't have to face. It is where a company backed by venture capital fails to meet its original targets. The venture capitalist must then decide if the company is worth continuing to back in which case another tranche of money is forthcoming, or the decision is made to pull the plug.

Early Stage Finance
The provision of venture capital right at the beginning of the life of a business, either to fund research and development, or the production of a prototype, or to set the business up so it can begin trading. Early stage finance is the most risky form of venture capital because failure rates are high and it may be many years before the investment can be realized.

Earn Outs   see *Ratchets*.

Equity Finance
Equity is another word for company share. Equity finance is when a company raises money by selling shares. The owners of these shares then become part owners of the company and are entitled to any dividends which the company might pay.

Exit

The point at which the venture capitalist exits from a company. If the company is successful this is normally when it goes public or is sold on to another company, although it may also arrange to buy its own shares from the venture capitalist.

Expansion Finance

Companies which have financed the early stages of their development from bank borrowings alone may find their banks unwilling to finance the next stage and may need to sell a stake in their company to a venture capitalist in order to fund expansion.

Hands-Off

A 'hands-off' relationship is where investors take no active part in the management of a company in which they have invested.

Hands-On

The opposite of 'hands off', a 'hands-on' relationship is where investors do play a part in the management of the companies in which they have invested. UK venture capitalists are increasingly following the North American example and assuming an active role in the companies in which they invest either by appointing new senior executives, or by insisting on nominating at least one non-executive directors.

Heads of Agreement

The draft agreement between a company and a venture capitalist which sets out the terms of the deal. The agreement is not binding except it may require the company to stop negotiating with others for a specified period, often called the 'lock out' period.

Independents

Venture capital operations which are owned independently and are not part of another financial institution, such as a bank, pension fund or life insurance company. Independents are responsible for raising their own investment funds; they cannot rely on a flow of funds being provided by one financial institution.

Internal Rate of Return (IRR)

The rate of return from an investment taking capital growth and dividend income into account. The calculation venture capitalists use to determine the price at which they will do a deal. For example, a high risk start up company will be required to make a high IRR, because the small number of successes in this sector must pay for all the failures. The provision of replacement finance, on the other hand, in a profit-making company will be priced with reference to a lower IRR because the risk is low.

Investment trust

A closed end fund. Authorized investment trusts are exempt from capital gains tax. The Association of Investment Trust Companies lists 22 UK-quoted specialist venture capital investment trusts.

Later Stage Finance

The provision of funds to established companies mainly for expansion. However, it can also include providing funds for entrepreneurs who want to get money out of their company at a time when it is not yet ready to be sold or go public, and the financing of companies which have fallen on hard times but which are reckoned to be due for a recovery. The risks of later stage finance are not as high as for early stage finance and the capital returns are not as great. However, part of the return will come in the form of income as most companies will be paying dividends.

Lemons and Plums

In venture capital the bad investments go wrong before the good investments take off, ie the lemons ripen before the plums.

Letter of Offer

The letter the entrepreneur receives once the venture capitalist has decided that it would like to invest and the rough details of the deal have been worked out. It is only at this stage that the lawyers get involved and start drafting the legal agreement which starts with the Heads of Agreement. An offer letter doesn't mean the entrepreneur will actually get the money in the end.

Living Dead

Venture capital funds hope they won't invest in too many of these – companies which are making modest profits but are going nowhere in particular.

Management Buy-In (MBI)

The same as a management buy-out except the deal is put together by a new management team, rather than the existing one, and it is this new management team which goes in to run the company if the MBI is successful. MBIs are financed in exactly the same way as MBOs.

Management Buy-Out (MBO)

The process by which the existing managers buy the company they work for. Most MBOs are smaller companies buying their way out of larger companies either because the larger company needs to raise cash or the activity no longer fits the corporate plan. In recent years there have been an increasing number of managers who have bought their companies from the receiver after the parent company has gone into receivership. The managers pay for their companies by borrowing money from the bank and selling shares to a venture capitalist.

Mezzanine Finance

High risk loans which, if included in the financing of a MBO or MBI, allow the deal to be structured in a way which gives the management the biggest possible stake in the company. Mezzanine finance is more expensive than borrowing money from the bank because the risks are higher. The presence of mezzanine finance was a common feature of the highly leveraged MBOs of the late 1980s many of which either failed or had to be restructured after failing to meet their interest payments.

Money Out

This is when the venture capitalist agrees to acquire shares directly from the entrepreneur. This is one way in which entrepreneurs get money out of their companies if they are not yet ready to be sold or floated on the stock market. 'Money out' transactions do not provide new money for the company.

Offer for Sale
One way of getting shares listed on the stock market. With this method, a company's shares are offered to the public at a fixed price through a prospectus which will be published in the national newspapers. If the shares are popular, investors won't get all the shares they asked for. If the offer fails to attract enough investors, the shares are left with the city institution which agreed to underwrite the issue.

Open Ended
Where the amount of money the venture capitalist has to invest is not determined in advance by the amount of money raised for a particular fund. Captive venture capital funds may be able to rely on a regular, or open ended, flow of money from their parent bank, pension fund or merchant bank.

Passive Funds   *see Hands-off.*

Placing
When a company arranges to go public by selling some or all of its shares to a number of institutions at an agreed price. The institutions are then free to sell them on the stock market or continue to hold them as an investment.

Price/Earnings Ratio (PE)
A measure of investor confidence. The PE ratio is the number of years a company would take to earn its share price. For example if a company has earnings per share of 10p and a share price of 100p, the PE ratio is 10. By and large, the higher the PE ratio, the better the company.

Rachets
Also known as 'earn outs', this is a way of structuring a venture capital deal to give the entrepreneur a higher stake in his or her business if they meet or exceed their performance targets.

Replacement Finance
A type of later stage finance which is used to buy out shareholdings, normally in family businesses, on the retirement or death of a senior manager. Called replacement finance because it replaces existing financing and doesn't involve the injection of any new capital.

S-Curve
There is a stage at which budding entrepreneurs can no longer finance the development of a product or service from their own resources and must seek outside finance before they can start selling. New enterprises are most at risk at this stage of their development. When these financing requirements are illustrated on a graph they appear as an elongated S – hence the name S-curve. Also known as the death valley curve.

Second Stage Finance see *Later stage finance*.

Seed Capital
Short for seed corn, this is the very early stage finance which can be in the form of loans or shares and is used to develop a business idea before it is ready to be commercially exploited. For example, it could fund research and development, the production of a proto-type or the development of a data base. *See Early stage finance.*

Share Incentive Scheme
A method of providing executives and/or employees with an incentive to work harder by awarding bonuses in the form of shares or the right to buy shares at a favourable price.

Share Quotation
When a company goes public and sells some or all of its shares to the public its shares are said to be 'quoted' or 'listed' and you can find out, either by looking in the newspaper, or by asking a stockbroker, how much the shares cost to buy and sell. Private company shares are unquoted and if shares change hands the price is by negotiation with the individual shareholder.

Small Ticket Equity
Small injections of equity capital of amounts less than around
£150 000 usually into start up companies. Venture capitalists are
traditionally reluctant to do such small deals because the cost
of due diligence and providing management support cannot be
justified on such small investments.

Start Up Finance
The finance to start a business once the research and development
and product development has been completed and there is a
product or service ready to be marketed.

Stock Market Listing
When a company goes public and sells its shares to the public, it's
shares are said to be 'listed' or 'quoted'. *See Share quotation.*

Sweat Equity
A venture capital deal where the management pays less for its
shares than the venture capitalist. It is a way of rewarding the
management for the 'sweat' that they have and will continue to
put into the business.

Subscription Agreement
A legal document outlining the terms under which the venture
capitalist is prepared to make the investment. Sometimes also
called the investment agreement.

Syndication
Any deal where there is more than one investor. Many large venture
capital deals, especially management buy-outs and buy-ins, are
syndicated by a so called 'lead' lender or venture capitalist who
will bring others in usually for a fee.

Tender Offer
Companies going public can either sell their shares at a fixed price
or they can effectively auction them by tender offer to the highest
bidders.

Trade Sale

The sale of a private company to another company. A trade sale is one of the main ways venture capitalists get their investments out of a particular company.

Turnaround Finance

Where the venture capitalist takes a stake in an ailing company in order to return it to profit. More common in the US than over here.

UK Limited Partnership

The main unquoted structure used by venture capitalists for raising investment funds. Limited partnerships normally have a limited life, often ten years, at the end of which the money is returned to investors.

Vulture Capital

A deal structured in such a way that it gives the venture capitalist an unfairly high stake in the company.

Yield

The income which an investment earns expressed as a percentage. For example a preference share priced at £100 paying an annual dividend of £5 is said to yield five per cent.

Bibliography

If you would like to read more about venture capital the following publications are recommended:

Business Plans and Financing Proposals, British Venture Capital Association, London, 1992.

Guide to Venture Capital, British Venture Capital Association, London, 1992.

Guide to Venture Capital in the UK & Europe, Lucius Cary (ed.), Venture Capital Report, Henley-on-Thames (*pub. biannually*).

Unquote, Initiative Europe, London (a fortnightly newsletter covering the venture capital industry).

Venture Capital Today, Tony Lorenz, Woodhead-Faulkner, Cambridge, 1985.

Who's Who in Risk Capital, Initiative Europe, London.

Useful Addresses

Further information on venture capital can be obtained from the following organizations:

British Venture Capital Association 3 Catherine Place, London SW1E 6DX *Tel*: 071 233 5212
This is the British trade association for venture capitalists in the UK. It publishes a Directory of Members and will provide free information, available in various publications (see previous page), on request.

Grosvenor Venture Managers Ltd Commerce House, 2–6 Bath Road, Slough, Berks SL1 3RZ *Tel*: 0753 811812

Initiative Europe 5–13 Bondway Business Centre, 71 Bondway, London SW8 1SQ *Tel*: 071 735 9838
Initiative Europe produces the 'Review of Institutional Investors', a specialist information service designed to assist independent fund managers with their fund raising.

3i Plc 91 Waterloo Road, London SE1 8XP *Tel*: 071 928 3131

Venture Capital Report Boston Road, Henley-on-Thames, Oxon RG9 1DY *Tel*: 0491 579999

Venture Economics The Quadrangle, 180 Wardour Street, London W1A 4YG *Tel*: 071 434 0411
Venture Economics publishes the *UK Venture Capital Journal*.

Index